Vietnam

Vietnam

BY TERRI WILLIS

Enchantment of the World
Second Series

Children's Press®

A Division of Scholastic Inc.

NEW YORK TORONTO LONDON AUCKLAND SYDNEY
MEXICO CITY NEW DELHI HONG KONG
DANBURY, CONNECTICUT

Frontispiece: A young Vietnamese girl

Consultant: Dr. Amy J. Johnson, Ph.D., Assistant Professor of History, Berry College, Mount Berry, Georgia

Please note: All statistics are as up-to-date as possible at the time of publication.

Book production by Herman Adler Design

Library of Congress Cataloging-in-Publication Data

Willis, Terri
    Vietnam / by Terri Willis
       p. cm. — (Enchantment of the world. Second series)
    Includes bibliographical references and index.
    ISBN 0-516-22150-7
    1. Vietnam—Juvenile literature. [1. Vietnam.] I. Title. II. Series.
DS556.3 .W53 2002
959.7—dc21   2001053758

Vietnam

Contents

Cover photo:
Women tying
crop bundles

One Pillar Pagoda

Young girls in
traditional clothes

A Country on the Move

ON THE RIVER THAT RUNS THROUGH THE VILLAGE, PED-dlers with their flat-bottomed sampam boats crowd near the shore. Brightly colored fruits and vegetables on board beckon to early shoppers. It's morning in Vietnam, and throughout the land people are rising and getting to work.

In the city, the rising sun casts long shadows from tall buildings, marking patterns on downtown areas that are beginning to fill with life. The bustling businesspeople move quickly on bicycle and on foot, making their way past the multitude of street vendors selling breakfast—coffee, a baguette, perhaps a steaming bowl of noodle soup. Miles away, in the countryside, farmers dressed in loose clothing and cone-shaped hats are already bent over their paddies, quietly and rhythmically planting the next crop of rice.

Vietnam is a vibrant and industrious country. Its people are building their economy for the new century and striving to leave behind a troubled, impoverished past for hopes of a promising future.

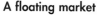

Opposite: **Planting rice**

A floating market

Vietnam is embracing technology.

A U.S. war veteran visiting a Vietnamese military cemetery

Not that the Vietnamese people can ever completely forget their long history, nor would they want to. Much of the country's culture, art, food, architecture, and religion are steeped in rich traditions developed over thousands of years. And many people still live and work in rural areas where little has changed for generations.

But in the urban areas, Vietnam is embracing industry and technology, struggling to become an economic leader in its part of the world. Lifestyles are changing, too, and residents enjoy modern conveniences and technology.

Some North Americans make a mistake when they think of Vietnam. To them, the word "Vietnam" usually only means a war; one that left a very ugly mark in American history. In fact, the North American involvement in the Vietnam War didn't even play a major part in the whole of that country's centuries of history. Vietnam's history goes back thousands of years. The war that we in North America refer to as the Vietnam War—to the Vietnamese, it's the American War—is just a short part of the nation's long story.

Indeed, the nation has had many difficulties. It has endured centuries of rule by foreign leaders. It has suffered centuries of poverty. During the Vietnam War, very serious environmental damage was done to its land. But Vietnam has worked hard to overcome its problems in the last two decades, and it has a new face to show to the world.

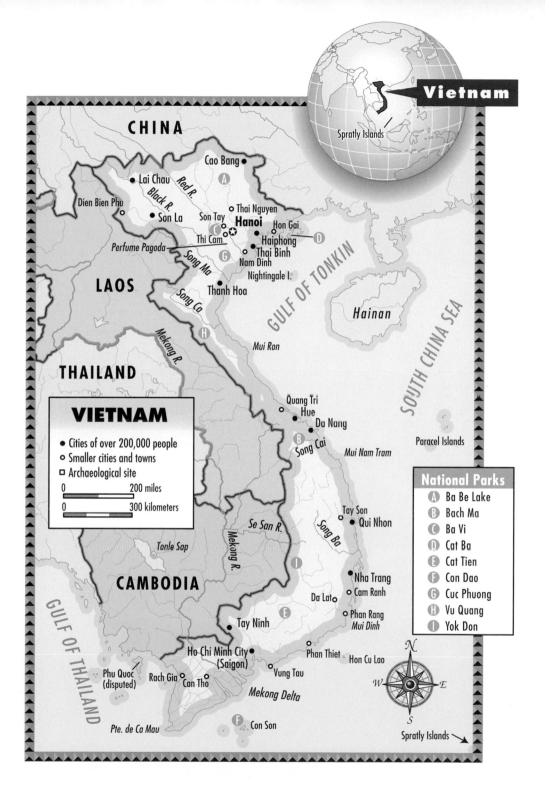

Vietnam

Spratly Islands

CHINA

Cao Bang •

• Lai Chau
Red R.
Dien Bien Phu
Black R.
• Son La
○ Son Tay ○ Thai Nguyen
Ⓒ **Hanoi** Hon Gai ○
Thi Cam □ ○ Haiphong Ⓓ
Song Ma Ⓖ • Thai Binh
Perfume Pagoda ○ Nam Dinh
Nightingale I.

LAOS
Song Ca
• Thanh Hoa
GULF OF TONKIN
Hainan

Ⓗ
Mui Ron

THAILAND
Mekong R.

Song Ma

SOUTH CHINA SEA

○ Quang Tri
○ Hue
• Da Nang
Ⓑ
Song Cai
Mui Nam Tram

Paracel Islands

VIETNAM

- Cities of over 200,000 people
- ○ Smaller cities and towns
- □ Archaeological site

| 0 | 200 miles |
| 0 | 300 kilometers |

Se San R.
Mekong R.

○ Tay Son
• Qui Nhon
Song Ba

Ⓘ

CAMBODIA
Tonle Sap

• Nha Trang
○ Cam Ranh
○ Da Lat
Ⓔ
○ Phan Rang
Mui Dinh

National Parks
Ⓐ Ba Be Lake
Ⓑ Bach Ma
Ⓒ Ba Vi
Ⓓ Cat Ba
Ⓔ Cat Tien
Ⓕ Con Dao
Ⓖ Cuc Phuong
Ⓗ Vu Quang
Ⓘ Yok Don

GULF OF THAILAND

• Tay Ninh

Ho Chi Minh City ●
(Saigon)
Phu Quoc
(disputed)
Rach Gia ○ ○ Can Tho
○ Vung Tau
Mekong Delta

○ Phan Thiet Hon Cu Lao

N
W E
S

Pte. de Ca Mau
Ⓕ ○ Con Son

Spratly Islands →

A Land
of Contrasts

V IETNAM STRETCHES OUT LONG AND ARCHING ALONG THE South China Sea. Forming an *s*, it has a large patch of land at the northern end, and another at the southern tip, separated by a long, narrow strip of mountains and coastline. North to south, Vietnam is 1,023 miles (1,650 kilometers) long, but little more than 31 miles (50 km) at its most slender east-west portion. Its widest spot in the north is 372 miles (600 km).

Vietnam shares borders with China in the north and with Laos and Cambodia in the west. Vietnam's territory also encompasses a vast sea area, including thousands of islands stretching from the Tonkin Gulf to the Gulf of Thailand. These islands include the disputed Spratly (*Quan Dao Thruong Xa*) and Paracel (*Hoang Sa*) islands, which China also claims.

Opposite: **Coastline near Da Nang**

A Land of Diversity

Vietnam's total land mass is 127,242 square miles (329,556 square kilometers). That's just a little bigger than the state of New Mexico. Though Vietnam is fairly small for a country, it contains great resources and a wonderful variety of environments and climates.

Vietnam has cool mountaintops, and shorelines graced by ocean breezes. Two major river deltas provide a wonderful environment for the rice paddies that help feed the country. Annual monsoons dump heavy rains on much of the country

A mountain valley in the northern highlands

for months, yet at other times Vietnam can be very dry. The south is tropical and almost always warm, but in the north, the temperatures can dip below freezing. You can find many different terrains and nearly any sort of weather in Vietnam.

Neighboring Countries

Vietnam is a part of a group of nations known as Indochina. Cambodia and Laos are the two other countries. A Danish mapmaker, Konrad Malte-Brun, gave the region this term in the early 1800s, and it applies to the knob of land south of China that plunges into the South China Sea. Vietnam makes up the entire eastern stretch of Indochina. All of Indochina is part of another regional grouping, Southeast Asia. There is great cultural and economic diversity within this region. Vietnam is, in many ways, reflective of the diversity found throughout Southeast Asia.

Three Regions of Vietnam

Vietnam has three different geographical regions. The northern region is known as Bac Bo, central Vietnam is Trung Bo, and the southern portion is Nam Bo.

Bac Bo

Many consider Bac Bo to be one of the most stunningly beautiful areas in the country. It is marked by high mountains to the north, which form the border between Vietnam and China. Farther south, lovely valleys and plateaus stretch to the very fertile Red River Delta area.

The population center here is Hanoi; with its 3.3 million residents, it is Vietnam's second-largest city and the nation's capital. About 90 percent of Bac Bo's population live in the delta, an important farming area.

The mountains to the north are the Hoang Lien Mountains. The nation's tallest peak is here—Phan Si Pan, at 10,312 feet (3,143 meters). Steep cliffs and waterfalls plunge to the rivers below. Green, thick jungles fill the valleys. These mountains played a major role in Vietnam's history. They are very hard to cross, and so, for centuries, they kept out strong armies from the north in China. Even today, the difficult terrain keeps the population low—only a few hill tribes make their homes in these mountains. Many geologists believe that this area could be rich in underground mineral deposits, but so far, not much mining has occurred.

Few people live in the Hoang Lien Mountains.

The Red River begins its 248-mile (400-km) journey to the Gulf of Tonkin in the South China Sea in China's Yunnan region. As the river approaches Vietnam's coastal lowlands, it fans out like spread fingers to create a delta region. The delta covers more than 5,750 square miles (15,000 sq km). This soggy delta land, a prime growing spot for rice, floods regularly because of silt that washes down the river. Over the ages, the river deposited silt in the low-lying riverbeds, raising their level. Many earthen dikes, some built more than 2,000 years ago, hold the water back. People have dug canals to channel the water into the rice paddies for irrigation. But during the monsoon season, between May and October, the heavy rains still cause flooding in the region.

The Red River

A waterfall in Trung Bo

Trung Bo

Trung Bo, Vietnam's central region, is a slender strip of land between the South China Sea to the east, and the Truong Son mountain range to the west. In the high mountain plateaus, there are towering limestone peaks along the border with Laos. More than 200 rivers have cut deep valleys through these mountains and plunge over steep waterfalls as they flow toward the South China Sea.

Visiting a cave temple in the
Marble Mountains

As the land sweeps downward toward the sea, dunes and
lagoons dot the coastal landscape. The bulk of the land is rich soil
formed by volcanic deposits from centuries ago. Farmers in this
region grow tea and coffee. Timber is cut by forestry operations.

Da Nang, Vietnam's fourth-largest city, home to about
375,000 people, is located here. Just outside Da Nang are five
special hills known as the Marble Mountains. Tucked away
high in these hills are dozens of caves containing statues

Looking at Vietnam's Cities

Ho Chi Minh City (pictured), Vietnam's largest city, is full of visual delights. There are many sights that show the city's rich history and culture. It covers an area of 910 square miles (2,356 sq km), and is home to some 5.2 million people. Ho Chi Minh City is one of the world's most densely populated places, with more than 52,000 people per square mile (20,000 per sq km).

It was founded in the 1700s by Vietnamese refugees fleeing from war farther north. When Vietnam was temporarily divided into North and South Vietnam, from 1954 to 1976, Ho Chi Minh City, then known as Saigon, was the capital of South Vietnam. The city is named for the leader of North Vietnam, Ho Chi Minh. The name means "he who enlightens."

The city's broad, tree-lined streets wind through many lovely residential areas, with homes built in French Colonial style. The Cholon district is home to many of the country's ethnic Chinese.

Business districts bustle with activity. The delicious foods of the region can be prepared with goods purchased at Ben Thanh Market. This is the largest of the city's several markets, where vegetables and fruits can be found, along with meat, poultry, and fish.

There are two major universities in Ho Chi Minh City, many museums, an excellent zoo, and many fine restaurants and theaters. Temples, shrines, churches, and pagodas throughout the city point to the religious diversity of the community.

Haiphong, in the north, is a city that has a population of about 1.5 million people. It had its beginnings as a quiet fishing village, but during the seventeenth century it became an important port because it was located near the capital city of Hanoi. Today it remains a busy seaport city, located near the Gulf of Tonkin on the Red River Delta. Here, natural resources such as coal and zinc are mined. A large cement factory is found just outside the city. Many visitors are pleasantly surprised at how lovely and well preserved much of the city is, despite its centuries of heavy military activity. Here one can find several churches, hotels, a theater, a museum, and gardens.

Da Nang is a major city in east central Vietnam. Built along the South China Sea on a large, protected bay, it is Vietnam's most important port. It is here where the U.S. Navy and other military stationed themselves during the war. Many beautiful beaches line the shores nearby. Cham Museum is a popular attraction in Da Nang. It houses a large selection of sculptures from the ancient kingdom of Champa, once located in the same region. Da Nang's population is about 375,000.

Hue is located in central Vietnam, and is in an area that was settled in the third century B.C. Today it is an important trade center. Textiles and cement are manufactured here; however, tourism is a major economic activity. Hue was capital of the Nguyen dynasty throughout the 1800s and early 1900s, therefore many historical royal and religious buildings can be found. The huge citadel is located here. Built in the early nineteenth century, the citadel contains the Imperial City, including royal palaces, parks, and temples. There is a prominent flag tower and nine sacred cannons. The cannons represent the four seasons and the five ritual elements of water, wood, metal, earth, and fire.

Because of it's many ancient royal buildings, fine museums and cathedrals, and stunning architecture, along with pretty lakes and lush vegetation, Hue, with a population of 265,000, is often considered one of Vietnam's most beautiful cities.

of Buddha. Some of these statues are believed to have magical powers. Many consider that each of the Marble Mountains stands for a special element of the universe—earth, gold, fire, wood, and water. Because of these ancient beliefs, these caves in the Marble Mountains are the site for many Buddhist religious ceremonies.

Nam Bo

The Mekong River flows for 2,597 miles (4,180 km) to its destination in the Mekong Delta of southern Vietnam and, finally, to the South China Sea. The Mekong fans out into a

A view of the Mekong River Delta from the space shuttle *Challenger*

The Back-Flowing River

The Red River causes serious flooding problems in Bac Bo each year during the monsoon season. But flooding during that season is rarely severe in the Mekong River Delta. Something unusual happens to the Mekong River as its water level starts to rise. It actually flows backward into the Tonle Sap Lake in Cambodia. Water from this large lake usually flows into the Mekong as it passes nearby on its way to the sea. During the monsoons, the lake holds most of the water that would otherwise spill over the riverbanks and cause flooding.

Islands

Along with the three main regions of Vietnam, the country claims the islands near its shore. Several of these islands are found in Halong Bay, located just off the Mekong River Delta. More islands are found farther out in the sea. Ownership of many of these islands is often disputed, with several countries claiming them.

The Spratly Islands are a group of about 100 islands, with a total land surface of less than 5 square miles (13 sq km), in the middle of the South China Sea. These islands are mainly uninhabited. Oil and fish are resources here, so many countries want to claim these islands. The Philippines, Taiwan, China, Malaysia, and Vietnam argue over ownership.

low shelf of soil and mineral deposits that have washed down into the river's mouth, forming a delta that is more than 29,000 miles square (75,000 sq km). These deposits continue to build, and push the land of south Vietnam into the sea by about 247 feet (75 m) each year. Here, thousands of rice paddies provide food for much of the country. The river itself is an important route for transporting goods throughout the region. Hundreds of farmers travel from place to place to sell their produce from small boats called *sampans*.

Climate

Vietnam's weather can be summed up by answering one of two questions: Is it wet? Or is it dry? Each year the monsoon season brings an average of 72 inches (183 m) of rain to the nation during the summer months of May through October.

Bike travel during the wet monsoon season

Vietnam's climate is dominated by winds called *monsoons* that change with the seasons. There are monsoons in the winter, which bring dry winds southward, originating from over the cold land moving toward the warmer Pacific and Indian Oceans. Dry monsoons keep clouds away. As the higher temperatures of summer warm the Asian mainland more quickly than the ocean waters, the winds shift. The cooler air from over the oceans blows northward over the land, and carries with it plenty of moisture. As the air warms over the warmer land, the moisture falls as rain. This is the wet monsoon season.

In Vietnam, temperatures vary between the north and south. It's cooler in the north, where the average temperature from November to April is 58° Farenheit (14.4° Celcius) when the dry monsoons are blowing over the area. When the wet monsoons shift into gear, from May to October, the temperature warms up, with average summer temperatures reaching 90°F (32.2°C) in the warmest period around July.

It gets even warmer in the south, with highs reaching up to 95°F (35°C) and beyond during the wet monsoons. During the cooler dry monsoons of winter, temperatures only go down to an average of about 70°F (21.1°C).

In the central region, *typhoons*, severe tropical hurricanes, sometimes hit the coastal plains. The wind and waves hit the beaches and coastline with tremendous force. They destroy boats, homes, businesses, and wildlife. Farther inland on the central highlands, destruction from typhoons is not a threat. But very heavy rains fall—an average of 130 inches (330 cm) per year—during the wet monsoons.

Monsoon

Mausim is the Arabic term for "season." The word *monsoon* comes from this term. It is unpleasant to live through months and months of nearly constant rain. However, Vietnamese people welcome the wet monsoons because the water helps grow crops that are vital to feeding the population.

This highway was washed out by heavy rains.

In 1999, typhoons and heavy rains caused severe damage to Vietnam's central coast. Two major floods within two months caused more than 700 deaths and left hundreds of thousands of people homeless. In some places, more than 40 inches (102 cm) of rain fell in four days. Monsoon rains were particularly heavy again in 2000, causing flooding in the Red River and Mekong deltas. Though these areas always flood during monsoons, this time it was particularly severe, damaging the dikes and canals and harming the region's important rice paddies.

Vietnam's Geographical Features

Highest Elevation: Phan Si Pan, 10,312 feet (3,143 m)

Lowest Elevation: Sea level, along the coast with the South China Sea.

Greatest Distance North to South: 1,023 miles (1,650 km)

Greatest Distance East to West: 372 miles (600 km)

Least Distance East to West: About 31 miles (50 km)

Longest River: The Mekong River, 2,597 miles (4,180 km)

Longest Mountain Chain: Truong Son, 800 miles (1,287 km)

Highest Average Temperatures: 85°F (29.4°C)

Lowest Average Temperature: 62°F (16.7°C)

Highest Average Annual Precipitation: 78 inches (198 cm), the Mekong Delta

Lowest Average Annual Precipitation: 66 inches (168 cm), the Red River Delta

Great Diversity

W ITH ITS GREAT DIVERSITY OF ECOSYSTEMS, RANGING from chilly mountains to warm seacoasts, soggy marshes to hot, lush jungles, it is no real surprise that Vietnam is home to a wide assortment of plants and animals. There are thousands of types of plants, and 770 bird species fill the air. At least 275 types of mammals are found in the country, along with 180 reptiles, 80 amphibians, and about 2,500 species of fish. Since not all the country has been explored by biologists, there may yet be even more. In fact, in the early 1990s, two new species of large mammals were discovered. Along with the wealth of plants and animals in Vietnam comes the harsh reality that many of them are endangered.

Plants

Only about 7,000 of Vietnam's plants have been identified to date. Some 2,300 are considered valuable for human use. Many are used for food; others are useful as medicines, timber, and furniture. Still others are good as animal fodder.

Rice is Vietnam's main crop. Bamboo, bananas, pineapple, and coconut grow wild in Vietnam, but they have also been cultivated and grown as cash crops.

Opposite: **The panther is one type of big cat that lives in Vietnam.**

Bamboo grows tall along this country road.

More than 1,500 types of woody plants—trees, shrubs, and vines—grow in Vietnam. Different kinds of trees grow at different elevations. In the high mountain ranges, hardwoods abound—mahogany, teak, oak, and ebony. At lower altitudes, pines and other evergreens are plentiful. Vines, such as rattan and liana, are found in the south and central regions. In the north, bamboo thickets are common in the middle mountain elevations. Along the coast are palms and swamps of mangrove trees, which grow in seawater. Grasses and sedges live in the delta regions.

Flowers and shrubs grow well in the country's warmer regions. Orchids thrive and are harvested to be sent around the world. Epiphytes, which are flowering vines that receive nutrients from the air and rain, live in rain forests. They depend on trees for support, reaching high to the top branches, where they can receive abundant sunlight and moisture.

Orchids grown in Vietnam are sold around the world.

Even Vietnam's cities are filled with growing things. Ho Chi Minh City is alive with color when its many tamarind trees are in bloom. Their red and yellow flowers brighten the streets. And bougainvillea, with flowers of purple and red, add color throughout the city as well.

The muntjac is a type of deer.

Animals

An amazing array of animals roam the lands and waters of Vietnam. There are large mammals—elephants, wild oxen, and bears. Several types of deer and big cats such as panthers, leopards, and tigers live here also. Other mammals include wild oxen, wild pigs, tapirs, mongooses, skunks, hares, porcupines, jackals, otters, and wildcats. Primates include macaques, langurs, gibbons, and rhesus monkeys. Squirrels, mice, and rats are common in the cities. The main domesticated animals in Vietnam are dogs and cats, pigs, cattle, goats, ducks, chicken, and water buffalo. Vietnam's reptiles

A langur

Gecko and tourists in Tam Dao National Park

Hundreds of bird species live in Vietnam.

include crocodiles, snakes such as pythons and cobras, and several kinds of lizards. Geckos are very common lizards, while monitor lizards and flying lizards are some of the more unusual reptiles of Vietnam.

The variety of fish found in Vietnam's rivers and along the seacoast is important to the fishing industry. The main fish include carp, catfish, tuna, mackerel, tilapia, and snakehead. Shellfish include crab, shrimp, and lobster. Fishers also catch squid, cuttlefish, and abalone.

Nearly 600 different kinds of birds are found in southern Vietnam, with a total of more than 770 when birds from the northern part of the country are included. Though birds are found throughout the country, most congregate in the deltas and along the coasts, especially storks, herons, and egrets, along with several types of ducks and cormorants. Other birds include hornbills, laughing thrushes, and brown hawk owls.

Sarus cranes are an environmental success story in Vietnam. This beautiful bird dances elaborately to attract a mate. During the Vietnam War, its habitat in the wetlands along the Cambodian border was ruined. American solders had drained the marshes and dropped herbicides in order to flush out enemy Viet Cong soldiers. After the war, the local government worked to restore the wetlands. The first Sarus cranes returned in 1986, and today there are more than 1,000 of them.

National Parks

Vietnam began establishing national parks to conserve wildlife in 1962, sooner than most countries in Indochina. All these parks feature terrific scenery and great animal watching, but most aren't very accessible so travelers have difficulty getting into the interiors.

Ancient trees and rare plants and animals are just a few of the attractions at Cuc Phuong, Vietnam's first national park. It was created in 1962. Cuc Phuong is in the mountains, bordering the provinces of Ninh Binh, Thanh Hoa, and Hoa Binh. With more than 77 square miles (200 sq km) of rain forest, Cuc Phuong is a refuge for many rare species of animals. Leopards and tigers live high in the mountains. Farther down the slopes, visitors may glimpse a slender, long-tailed delacour langur, an endangered monkey. Other rare species include fish that live only in underground rivers and unusual red-bellied squirrels. Trees more than 1,000 years old grow in the park. Woody vines, called lianas, grow more than a half-mile (a kilometer) long. The park is most beautiful in spring, when the hillsides are colored by masses of blooming flowers and thousands of butterflies fill the sky.

Vietnam's largest wildlife preserve is Yok Don National Park in Dak Lak Province, 143,000 acres (58,000 hectares) of lush forest and mountains. While the scenery surrounding Yok Don Mountain is beautiful, the animals draw most visitors. In fact, there's more biological diversity here than in any other region of Indochina. About 200 types of birds live here, including peacocks. Mammals include bears, leopards, and tigers (including the rare Indochinese tiger). Best known, though, are the Indian elephants. Today few

wild elephants live here—hunters and illegal poachers have cleared them out over the past several centuries. However, visitors can still ride elephants and travel deep into the jungle.

The Cat Tien National Park in Dong Nai Province is notable for another large inhabitant, the Javan rhinoceros (pictured). This is one of the rarest creatures in the world—about 10 exist. Javan rhinos live only in this park and in a park in Indonesia.

One of the smallest national parks in Vietnam is home to more unusual wildlife. Cat Ba National Park, at only 37,000 acres (15,000 ha), is located on an island in the South China Sea, about 12 miles (20 km) off the coast of Haiphong. It was established in 1986 to protect the diverse ecosystem off its shore. There are colorful coral reefs and pretty mangrove swamps. A rare type of snub-nosed monkey, the golden-headed langur, is found in this park and only in four other places in the world. These monkeys live on the limestone cliffs found along the shoreline.

Late in the last century, scientists were excited by two amazing discoveries: in 1992 the Vu Quang ox, also known as the saola; and in 1994, the giant muntjac, which is similar to a deer. These two large mammals had been living in a remote forest for centuries without being known to anyone but local villagers. In the Vu Quang Nature Reserve, where these discoveries were made, scientists also discovered a new species of river carp and a type of deer species related to the barking deer.

These animals had been unknown because they are so rare, and they were quickly added to Vietnam's lengthy list of endangered species. More than eighty mammals and ninety birds are on the lists of endangered species in Vietnam.

The Vu Quang Ox

When a never-before-documented animal was discovered living in Vietnam in 1992, it created quite a stir among biologists! The Vu Quang ox is the largest and most unexpected living mammal species to be discovered in more than fifty years. It took a few years for scientists to actually see the ox, even after they knew it existed. Scientists first discovered its unusual horns—horns that were long, straight, and smooth, unlike any ever documented before. These horns gave the Vu Quang ox its other name, saola, because it is also the local Vietnamese term for "weaving spindle," which the horns resemble. From local hunters, scientists obtained some skulls and other bones, as well as three complete skins, showing dark brown fur with a black stripe down its back and white markings on its face. They knew it was in the same animal family with cattle and gazelle, but they couldn't locate a live one. They set up cameras to take pictures, but had no luck.

Finally, in 1994, a local hunter captured a female saola, about five months old, and turned it over to authorities. Soon a young male was captured. Unfortunately, both died a few months later from respiratory and digestive problems. Scientists knew so little about these creatures that they were unable to save them.

Since then, a few more saolas have been spotted, though no one knows exactly how many there are. Vietnamese authorities are working hard to save them. They are trying to protect their habitat and to encourage the local villagers not to hunt these rare creatures.

The kouprey, or grey ox, is one of Vietnam's many endangered species. Weighing in at 1,500 to 2,000 pounds (700 to 900 kilograms), it is a grazer that lives on the grasses and leaves of the country's open savannas, as well as on evergreen and deciduous trees. It is one of the rarest surviving large mammals in the world, but it has been threatened by over-hunting and loss of habitat. When they were first discovered in 1937, about 2,000 of these creatures existed. Today, there may be as few as 100.

The rarest large mammal in the world is the Javan rhinoceros. Though it once lived throughout Southeast Asia, this rhino now lives only along the Dong Nai River of south-central Vietnam and in one small area of Indonesia. Only about 10 survive.

A captured sun bear for sale

The clouded leopard is another endangered species living in Vietnam's northern jungles and forests. Its numbers are declining because its habitat is being destroyed, but mostly because of hunting. Even though it is illegal to sell its fur, sales continue. Clouded leopard fur is prized in Taiwan—a leopard jacket is a symbol of power and wealth.

The sun bear and Asiatic black bear are also threatened due to loss of habitat and illegal hunting. While both are captured and sold as pets, more are killed. Their gall bladders are considered delicacies that contain power to strengthen those who eat them. In Thailand, bear paw soup is popular, and a single bowl can cost the equivalent of several hundred U.S. dollars. Sumatran rhinoceros, found in Vietnam, are killed for their horns, which are used as a medicine in some Asian countries.

Among Vietnam's other endangered mammal species are the Indian elephant, concolor gibbon, and the hairy-nosed otter. The orange-necked partridge and the black-hooded laughing thrush are some endangered birds found only in Vietnam. Endangered reptiles and amphibians include the Annam leaf turtle and the Vietnamese salamander.

This captured Indian elephant is used as a work animal.

Many of Vietnam's plants are distinctive forms, too, found only within small areas of Vietnam, leaving them open to quick extinction if their ecosystem is damaged. The country has suffered serious ecological damage, particularly due to war and poor management of resources.

Environmental Problems

During the Vietnam War in the 1960s and early 1970s, the U.S. military sprayed Agent Orange over approximately one-fifth of Vietnam's land. This spray is a defoliant, a chemical compound containing the poison dioxin, that was used to kill leaves and strip trees bare. It made it impossible for enemy soldiers to hide from aircraft beneath the heavy jungle canopy. Entire forests dried up and died; many eventually were burned. Mangrove forests were particularly hard-hit. Thousands of farmers' crops were damaged, leaving the local people hungry. Millions of wild and domesticated animals died.

Dioxin remains in the environment for a long time, and Vietnam's natural areas still have not recovered completely. Other problems still linger from the war. Armies used special plows to cut down wide swaths of trees to clear areas for military bases,

An abandoned military airstrip

and the 13 million tons (11.8 million metric tons) of bombs dropped caused damage beyond their obvious explosive power. Thousands of gaping holes remain on the terrain, and the soil around them is so compacted from the blasts that little can grow there.

Since the war, new problems have emerged that continue to damage the environment. Because of the country's growing population, the demand for farmland has increased, therefore more forests are being cut. Trees are also being used for fuel and for building. The loss of habitat seriously harms the animals who live in these forests. Prior to the war, 43 percent of Vietnam's land was covered by forest. Today, it is less than 19 percent. More than half the nation's forests have been lost.

Repairing the Damage

Vietnam's Ministry of Forestry is working to replant trees on much of the land that was damaged during the war. The ministry is replacing vegetation along the seacoast and adding trees to bare hills in the nation's midsection. Farmers are also being encouraged to plant fruit trees as crops, and schoolchildren are getting into the act as well by planting and caring for millions of trees. Popular tree-planting programs revolve around important holidays.

The government has made it illegal to do several things that are harmful to the environment. Certain farming practices that require clearing lots of land have been stopped, and, instead, the government offers financial support to farmers who plant trees.

Police are cracking down on illegal hunting and trade, too, in the hopes of slowing the decline of several endangered species. Trading ports are being watched more carefully to see that illegal animal items are not being sold to other countries. While Vietnam is a land of great biological diversity, there is also a lot of adversity. Years of war, poverty, and mismanagement have taken their toll. Vietnam's government recognizes the environmental problems the country faces and is taking some steps to solve them.

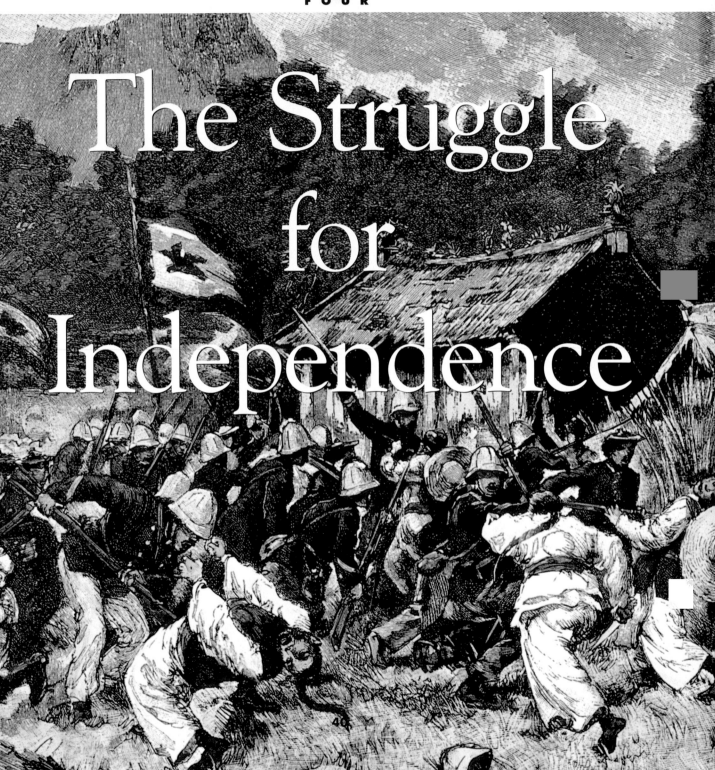

The Struggle for Independence

ANY OF VIETNAM'S CITIZENS DESCENDED FROM THE same group—the early inhabitants of the Ma River Valley in northern Vietnam. Those original settlers, from southern China and eastern Indochina, came to the region some 300,000 years ago, during the Paleolithic Age when pre-historic humans were just learning to use stone tools. Gradually they developed agricultural skills, learning to cultivate rice by using canals and irrigation.

Opposite: **French attack Indochina during the nineteenth century**

A bronze ax head of the Dong Son people

Over many centuries, they developed into the Dong Son people, a fairly sophisticated culture during the Bronze Age, around 3000 B.C. They used bronze to create tools and weapons. Eventually, they become known as People of the Valley, *Lac Viet*, and inhabited nearly all of the Red River Delta. Bronze drums discovered in the 1920s were created by the Lac Viet and used for religious rituals. Today, these drums are important evidence that this first, truly independent Vietnamese culture did exist.

As the population grew during the following centuries, it expanded down the coast. This movement was known as *Nam Tien*, or "March to the South." But before this southward march was to be completed, the people of the region had to fight off centuries of aggressors.

Beginning around 250 B.C., Chinese warlords were the first to conquer parts of the region. The Vietnamese held on to their independence until 111 B.C. Then the Han emperors of China took control of the entire Red River Delta, and China maintained its hold for a thousand years. The Chinese stronghold began in northern Vietnam, near the Chinese border, and moved southward over the years.

Southeast Asia, 800

State societies   Empires   Farming societies

The Chinese set up a feudalistic system. Upper-class rulers controlled the local population and demanded heavy tribute, or payments, from the Vietnamese. Chinese control became more powerful as the years went on, and the Chinese influence on Vietnam's culture grew strong. Some influences were positive—the Chinese instituted new technology for silk production and hydraulic works. They introduced writing to the Vietnamese. But through it all, the Vietnamese people were struggling to hold on to their own identity. During the long period of Chinese domination, Vietnamese peasants rebelled and had periods of independence, but each was short-lived. In A.D. 939 a Vietnamese rebellion was finally strong enough to defeat the Chinese.

The Trung Sisters

Would you be surprised to learn that the biggest heroes of Vietnam's rebellions against China were women— the Trung sisters? The Chinese murdered Trung Trac's husband in A.D. 40. He had been plotting against the Chinese. This drove Trac into action. Trac, with her sister, Nhi, gathered support from local peasants and fought against the Chinese, forcing them out of Vietnam's northern region. Trung Trac became ruler for three years, until the Chinese sent in 20,000 troops to retake the area. The sisters managed to escape by jumping into a river. Though they were not able to bring permanent freedom to Vietnam, they left a powerful example for others to follow. They gave hope to those who would eventually gain freedom for the nation. Today they are honored throughout the country, and many streets are named for them.

For the thousand years that China controlled most of northern Vietnam, the southern portion was being heavily influenced by Indian culture. During the first century A.D., Indian sailors traveling from India to China established ports along Vietnam's southern coast, which became small kingdoms. The most famous kingdom was Champa. Here, religious kings ruled, bringing Buddhism to the region.

The Chinese tolerated these small kingdoms, though they did force them to pay taxes. But when the Vietnamese people freed themselves from Chinese rule, they wanted more control over the Indian kingdoms as well. Eventually, the entire region was brought under Vietnamese control.

Vietnam, on Its Own

Fighting continued in independent Vietnam, known then as *Nam Viet*. Now the fighting was between different groups of Vietnamese who wanted to lead the nation. Ngo Quyen, the leader of the 938 revolution, led for five years, until his death. Then twelve local warlords competed for control for another

The Dynasties of Vietnam

What is a dynasty? It is a family or group that holds power in a region for many years. Leadership of the country is passed from one family member to another in succession. In Vietnam, several dynasties ruled from 938 until 1954. Some dynasties were fairly brief, while others lasted many decades, causing great changes. During most of these dynasties, the emperors held supreme power. They made the laws, led the military, were in control of the justice system, and often led the religious affairs of the nation.

twenty-five years. Finally, in 968, Dinh Bo Linh became ruler and united the country. He resumed paying taxes to Chinese rulers in order to ensure that China would not invade Vietnam. These payments continued until the 1800s.

Stability finally came with the leadership of the Ly dynasty, which began in 1009 with Ly Thai To. He and his successors, who led for more than 200 years, established a capital city, Thang Long, in northern Vietnam. This city became the modern capital, which is now Hanoi. The dynasty improved the economy as it built sophisticated irrigation systems for growing rice, allowed more people to own land, and increased taxes. The country's first university, in Hanoi, was founded by a Ly king in 1076. Another Ly king built Vietnam's military into a strong force.

The Tran dynasty defeated the Ly dynasty in 1225. The Tran dynasty continued to increase the size of the country's armies. It was able to repel three major invasions by the Mongols, led by

Kublai Khan going into battle

Kublai Khan. But spending so much on the military left little money to improve the country. Northern Vietnam faced a serious famine during the late 1300s, and hungry peasants revolted. A new leader came in, but only for seven years. While the country was unstable, Chinese troops returned and took control.

This time the Chinese tried to weaken the Vietnamese by destroying their culture and the bonds that held them together. Literature, works of art, written accounts of history—much of it was destroyed. Chinese rulers made it illegal to practice local religious customs and traditions. China demanded high taxes to keep the Vietnamese poor. But unrest grew. A landowner, Le Loi, gathered soldiers in the mountains south of Hanoi and spent ten years fighting the Chinese. Le Loi and his troops drove the Chinese out in 1427.

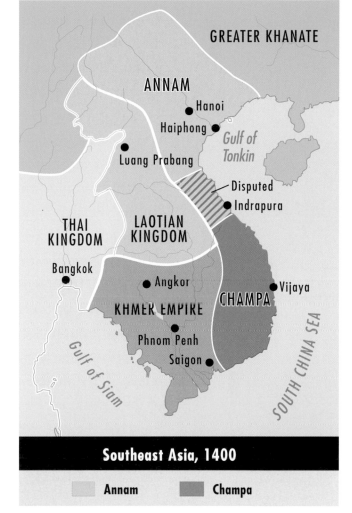

Le Loi became King Le Thai To, founder of the Le dynasty. One of his successors, Le Thanh Tong, who ruled from 1460 to 1497, was the greatest king of this dynasty. His agricultural reforms increased grain production. He opened up to the Vietnamese more land in the south that had been held by the kindgom of Champa. He organized the first census of the kingdom. His legal system became the basis for the country's judicial system for nearly 400 years. Changes brought by the Le dynasty created a new wave of prosperity in Vietnam.

Several newly wealthy landowners, jealous of the dynasty's power, wanted to obtain that control for themselves. They built up armies strong enough to challenge the dynasty. Two powerful families, the Nguyen and Trinh clans, at first helped the Le dynasty fight off the landowners' armies. In the end, the Nguyen and Trinh clans established their own territories. The Trinh family controlled the north from their headquarters in Hanoi. The Nguyen family, with their base in Hue, controlled all of southern Vietnam. Though the Le dynasty wasn't removed from its kingdom, it had no real power.

With the lack of central leadership, rulers found it easy to cheat. They made money for themselves while depriving most of their citizens of basic needs. There were a few wealthy families, but the rest were hungry. Vietnam's prosperity dwindled. Again, peasants rose up in anger. Their small rebellions were defeated for decades, until 1788, with the Tay Son Rebellion.

The Tay Son Rebellion

Aided by thousands of peasants, three brothers led the charge from their hometown of Tay Son. They took over property from wealthy landowners and divided it among the poor. With this their popularity grew. Eventually they conquered both the Nguyen and Trinh clans and brought an end to the Le dynasty. The country was again reunited for a time.

Nguyen Long, a member of the Nguyen clan, gathered his army together and began a long fight to regain control of the country. France, which had long wanted some involvement in Vietnam, supplied military assistance. After fourteen years, Nguyen was successful. The Nguyen dynasty, which he founded in 1802, lasted until 1954. It was Vietnam's final dynasty.

As emperor, Nguyen expressed a hatred of Christianity, which had come to Vietnam in the 1500s. His successor, Minh Mang, agreed. They felt threatened by Christian connections with France, fearing that France was attempting to increase its involvement in the region. Minh ordered the execution of thousands of Vietnamese Christians. No one knows for sure how many died. In the 1830s seven French missionaries in Vietnam were also killed. Many French citizens wanted their country to take military action against Vietnam.

Nine bronze urns in Hue represent the emperors of the Nguyen Dynasty.

French troops invading
Vietnam in 1858

French Control

French emporer Napoleon III ordered the invasion of
Vietnam in 1858. France's desire to increase its trade position
by controlling Vietnam, along with public sentiment against
Vietnam for the missionary deaths, prompted the move. Over
eight years' time, French armies took control of more and
more of Vietnam's territory. By 1867, all of southern Vietnam
was under French rule, becoming a colony named Cochin
China. It took France until 1883 to take over all of Vietnam.
They named northern Vietnam Tonkin. The central portion
was called Annam.

Even though the Nguyen dynasty remained in the kingdom, it had no real power. The French controlled all aspects
of government in Vietnam. Though the French built roads,

railroads, harbors, and bridges throughout the country, these didn't benefit the Vietnamese people. The French used this infrastructure as a means to get at Vietnam's many natural resources. Coal, rice, and rubber were important resources for the French. The French promoted industry, too, but Vietnamese workers received low wages, and all profits went to France.

Hard Times for Vietnam

The Vietnamese people suffered under French rule. By 1940, approximately 15 percent of children went to school. About 80 percent of the population was illiterate (unable to read and write). Working conditions and pay were poor, and medical care was almost nonexistent. Resistance movements, groups of Vietnamese people planning ways to overthrow the French colonial government in Vietnam, were growing.

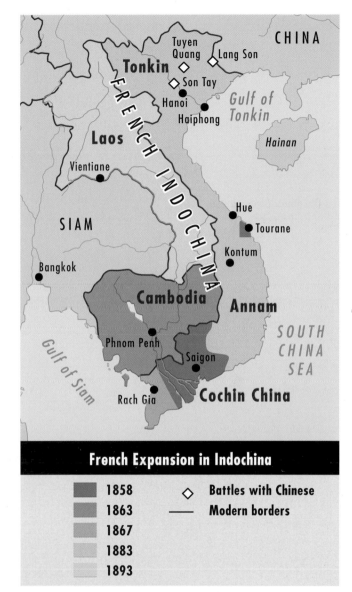

French Expansion in Indochina

▮ 1858	◇ Battles with Chinese
▮ 1863	─ Modern borders
▮ 1867	
▮ 1883	
▮ 1893	

In 1925, the Revolutionary Youth League of Vietnam was founded by Nguyen Ai Quoc. He later changed his name to Ho Chi Minh. He had a strong desire for his country to regain its independence. The success of his Youth League enabled him to enlist other groups. Together they formed the Indochinese Communist Party in 1930. This group called for peasant uprisings and gained political benefits for the Vietnamese people.

Japan Takes Control

Ho Chi Minh preparing to fight the French

In 1940, Germany invaded and took over France. At that time an agreement gave Vietnam to the Japanese, though the French were allowed to control the colonies. Japan used Vietnam as a major base for its military operations. In 1941, the Indochinese Communist Party saw this turmoil as a great opportunity to throw out both the Japanese and the French and gain independence for Vietnam. They established the Viet Minh, a special fighting force. Ho Chi Minh was its leader.

Because the United States had joined World War II against Japan, the Viet Minh began an

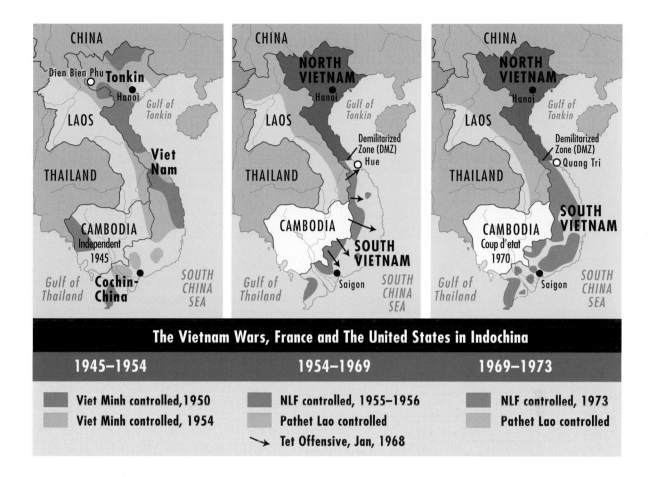

The Vietnam Wars, France and The United States in Indochina

1945–1954	1954–1969	1969–1973
Viet Minh controlled, 1950	NLF controlled, 1955–1956	NLF controlled, 1973
Viet Minh controlled, 1954	Pathet Lao controlled	Pathet Lao controlled
	Tet Offensive, Jan, 1968	

alliance with the United States. In 1945, the Japanese, severely beaten in the war, surrendered. Ho Chi Minh happily declared Vietnam's independence. The French, still wanting to control Vietnam, refused to accept Vietnamese independence and fought back.

France retained control of the south, while the Viet Minh were driven back into the northern portion of Vietnam. Ho sought help from the United States, but by that time, the United States had a policy to stop the spread of Communism.

Soldiers in the Battle of Dien Bien Phu

South Vietnamese president Ngo Dinh Diem

Though Ho had been a friend, he was also a communist. So the United States sent large amounts of money to France to help it regain control.

The Viet Minh didn't give up. In 1949, China's new communist government offered aid, and the fighting continued. In 1954, the Viet Minh made a successful attack on a French fortress during the Battle of Dien Bien Phu. It was a major defeat for the French. Tired of the war, France agreed to a settlement. This was the end of the Franco–Viet Minh conflict, called the First Indochina War.

Other world powers drew up a peace agreement called the Geneva Accords. The agreement was presented at the Geneva Conference held in Switzerland in 1954. Through this agreement, Vietnam was divided into two nations. North Vietnam was led by Ho Chi Minh and the Viet Minh. Hanoi was its capital. It received aid from China and the Soviet Union, both communist nations.

South Vietnam, with Saigon as the capital, was led by Emperor Bao Dai, the last emperor of the weakened Nguyen dynasty. He appointed Ngo Dinh Diem as prime minister. Ngo seized power and removed Bao Dai as head of state. Ngo became president of South Vietnam, which he named the Republic of Vietnam. It was backed financially by the United States.

Ho was not in the least satisfied with this arrangement. He wanted his entire country to be united. In 1960 his government established the National Liberation Front (NLF). Its military force was called the Viet Cong. The Viet Cong led many guerrilla attacks against Ngo's government. This was the beginning of the Vietnam War, also called the Second Indochina War.

Ngo was facing trouble from inside his own country as well. Conditions were poor throughout the nation, and the Viet Cong were able to take over many parts of the countryside. Ngo's popularity dwindled. In 1963, a military coup overthrew his government and he was killed. Political confusion followed. The United States decided to step in.

Vietnamese soldiers guarding Viet Cong prisoners in 1962

The United States Enters

In 1964, America claimed that a U.S. Navy ship had been attacked in international waters east of North Vietnam. President Lyndon Johnson ordered a major bombing raid on North Vietnam. Congress granted approval. Soon after, 3,500 U.S. Marines were sent to South Vietnam to assist in the fighting against the NLF. Most military leaders felt it would be a war that could quickly and easily be won in order to stop the spread of Communism throughout Southeast Asia.

But North Vietnamese leaders did not give up the fight. Large numbers of U.S. troops were sent to South Vietnam because the U.S. military was not doing well and needed to increase its numbers in order to try to win. Many South Vietnamese people felt that this was a civil war and were opposed to Americans being there. Many Americans felt the same. But U.S. leaders still sent more troops. About 75,000 U.S. soldiers were in Vietnam in July 1965—the number grew to 500,000 in early 1968. There were also about 600,000 South Vietnamese soldiers. The number of deaths rose rapidly, but the Viet Cong were slowly being driven out of South Vietnam.

U.S. soldiers entering a Vietnamese village

The Tet Offensive was North Vietnam's answer. It began in January 1968 during the Tet holiday, a new year's celebration. The Viet Cong launched attacks on every major South Vietnamese city and town, as well as strategic points in the countryside. The intense battles continued for weeks.

It was becoming clear that even with huge numbers of soldiers and military hardware, the United States couldn't win. In the United States, the peace movement was putting pressure on the government to end the war. President Johnson halted the bombing in the north and began negotiations with North Vietnamese leaders. The Paris Peace Talks, which began in 1968, included representatives from the South Vietnamese government as well.

Still, the fighting continued. Losses mounted on both sides. Johnson refused to run for reelection, and in 1968

Damage to Saigon during the 1968 Tet Offensive

Richard Nixon was elected president. He began to slowly pull American soldiers out of Vietnam. In the United States, public opinion was growing against the war. People on many college campuses and in cities and towns across the country protested America's involvement.

A peace treaty was signed in January 1973. U.S. troops were withdrawn, and a peaceful resolution of the conflict was to take place. But more than 100,000 North Vietnamese troops remained in South Vietnam, and the fighting continued long after the U.S. soldiers had left. In 1975, communist troops took control of Saigon and declared victory. The war had finally come to an end.

Communist troops occupied Saigon in 1975.

Vietnamese refugees in
Hong Kong

Vietnam Is Reunited

North Vietnam and South Vietnam were reunited on July 2, 1976. The country was renamed the Socialist Republic of Vietnam, led by a communist government with its capital in Hanoi. But the price had been high. More than 3 million Vietnamese had died. Much of the countryside had been damaged by the fighting. Wilderness had been destroyed, and villages had been burned. Many people were homeless and hungry.

Over the next several years, hundreds of thousands of people fled the country on boats. Known as the "boat people," they headed toward Hong Kong and other countries in Southeast Asia. Many eventually came to the United States. Some boat people escaped from South Vietnam as they feared persecution by the new government. Others just wanted to live in a place with greater prosperity and less destruction.

It was clear that the new government faced severe problems. The beloved leader Ho Chi Minh had died in 1969, and no strong leaders had taken his place. For so long the country had focused on war. Now, it was a challenge to deal with the issues that peacetime presented.

The economy was bad, and severe flooding in some parts, with drought elsewhere, increased the difficulties. Throughout the next decade, leaders tried to form alliances with the neighboring nations of Laos and Cambodia. In the end, Vietnam became involved in more fighting, as these countries dealt with their own internal strife. China, formerly a friend, attacked Vietnam in 1979 for its dealings in Cambodia. Vietnam was becoming isolated from nearly every other country in the world.

It was clear that changes were needed. The government announced a series of economic changes in the early 1980s, which led to the *doi moi* reforms of 1986. These reforms helped to open the Vietnamese economy to the rest of the world. Vietnamese people were eager to participate. The relaxed economic regulations and governmental controls gave them opportunities to run businesses on their own. They could build industries, trade with other nations, and promote tourism. They wanted to be part of the world economy and enjoy greater prosperity. Few held any lingering grudges regarding the war.

The United States ended its long-standing trade embargo, or trade restrictions, with Vietnam in 1994. The next year full diplomatic relations were established. In November 2000, President Bill Clinton traveled to Vietnam, the first president since Richard Nixon to visit there. He was greeted warmly by crowds, even in Hanoi. His mission was mainly to deal with the issue of servicemen still missing in action since the war. But his visit also served to increase trade between the two nations and to promote greater cooperation between the United States and Vietnam.

U.S. president Bill Clinton in Vietnam

Governing Vietnam

THOUGH VIETNAM'S HISTORY GOES BACK THOUSANDS OF years, its current constitution is only about a decade old. Approved in 1992, this constitution updated the one adopted in 1980. The constitution guides the decisions of the country's government.

At the head of Vietnam's government is the 450-member National Assembly, or *Quoc-Hoi*. It is unicameral, meaning that there is only one legislative house. Assembly members are elected to five-year terms by popular vote of citizens age eighteen and older. In turn, its members elect the president and vice president, who also serve five-year terms.

During its two annual sessions, the National Assembly considers legislation proposed by the executive branch of the government. Before 1992, the assembly basically "rubber-stamped" such proposals without much consideration. Since the new constitution was passed, the assembly holds much more power to make decisions on its own. It also is more willing to follow suggestions from citizens as guidance.

Opposite: **Members of the National Assembly at Ho Chi Minh's tomb**

A meeting of the National Assembly

NATIONAL GOVERNMENT OF VIETNAM

VIETNAMESE COMMUNIST PARTY

NATIONAL ASSEMBLY

PRESIDENT

PRIME MINISTER

VICE PRESIDENT

Cabinet

DEPUTY PRIME MINISTERS AND STATE ORGANIZATION HEADS

Vietnam's Full Name

The nation's full name is the Socialist Republic of Vietnam. In Vietnamese it is *Cong Hoa Xa Hoi Chu Nghia Viet Nam*, or Viet Nam for short. This name dates back to 1976 when the country united at the end of the Vietnam War.

The government includes a cabinet that is led by a prime minister. The prime minister is a member of the National Assembly who has been nominated by the president and approved by the National Assembly. Deputy prime ministers and state organization heads in the cabinet are appointed by the prime minister and approved by the National Assembly. These appointees direct such areas of national concern as water conservation, forestry, and agriculture. They also supervise the work of local governments.

At the local level, there are fifty provinces in Vietnam and three municipalities—Hanoi, Haiphong, and Ho Chi Minh City. Provinces and municipalities are further divided into some 500 districts. Leading the districts are People's Councils, elected by the people of the district. The councils name administrative committees to do the work. In making their decisions, these committees usually must follow the will of higher government officials and leaders of the Vietnamese Communist Party.

Most of the real power in Vietnam isn't held within the government structure—it is within the Vietnamese Communist Party. According to the constitution, this is the sole source of leadership for the country. It would be difficult for anyone from another political party to hold office. Though the president and the cabinet are in charge of running the government, policy decisions affecting the entire country are made by the Communist Party.

Communist Party delegates voting for a party leader

Ho Chi Minh

Ho Chi Minh was born in central Vietnam in 1890 and named Nguyen Sinh Cung. His father had been a civic leader but was forced out of his job for speaking out against the French colonists. Ho took part in a student protest and was kicked out of high school. He took a job as a deckhand on a cargo ship. After spending some time in the United States, and more in Great Britain, Ho settled in Paris.

Even though Ho no longer lived in Vietnam, his love for his country remained strong. He changed his name to Nguyen Ai Quoc, meaning "Nguyen the Patriot." He helped to found the French Communist Party in 1920. He was impressed by Communism in Russia, and in 1923 he moved there. But soon he was back closer to home, in southern China. He helped establish the first communist group in Vietnam—the Revolutionary Youth League.

In 1927, Ho was forced out of the country by Chinese leaders who were not communist. He moved to Thailand, where he hid as a Buddhist monk; he then moved to Hong Kong. All the while, he remained concerned with the situation in Vietnam. In 1941, he quietly moved back to his homeland. He was growing old and sickly, yet he spent his time hiding in damp caves in Vietnam's northern mountains. He led a band of guerilla fighters who used homemade weapons and booby traps in their struggle against the French. He was joined by some young leaders, and together they organized the League for the Independence of Vietnam, also known as the Viet Minh, a strong fighting unit. In 1954, they forced the French out.

Under the agreement signed during the Geneva Conference in 1954, Vietnam was split in half. Ho was elected president of communist North Vietnam. Ho believed the country should be united, but a competing government was set up in South Vietnam. For years, Ho pushed for reunification, but negotiations didn't work. This division set the stage for the Vietnam War that followed. Ho did not live to see the end of the war and the unification of the country. He died in 1969. Since his death, he has become the most revered of Vietnam's leaders.

Because the Communist Party is central to Vietnamese life, there are a number of organizations that give citizens a chance to become involved. Many women join the Vietnamese Women's Union. Children may belong to the Ho Chi Minh Communist Youth Union. Farmers may join the Farmer's Federation, and industrial workers may belong to the Vietnam Federation of Trade Unions.

Members of a communist youth group

All groups perform social and community projects. Politically active, they also serve as training grounds for members wishing to join the Communist Party.

Vietnam's Flag

The flag has a red background, with a yellow star that stands for communism. It was adopted in 1955 by North Vietnam and used as Vietnam's flag after reunification. The country's coat of arms also features the star, along with rice, denoting the importance of agriculture, and a gear, representing industry.

Defendants on trial in Hanoi People's Court

The Justice System

The court system in Vietnam has several levels that are similar to the courts in the United States and Canada. District courts are the lowest level in Vietnam. There is one district court in each of the more than 500 districts. The decisions made here may be appealed to a higher court at the city or provincial level. These courts each have a judge and group of citizens, called people's assessors, assigned to help decide cases. From here, decisions are appealed to the Supreme People's Court. Members of this court are appointed to five-year terms by the National Assembly.

A separate segment of Vietnam's justice system is the Supreme People's Office of Supervision and Control. It acts as a watchdog for the government, making sure that laws are carried out fairly. It monitors government agencies and watches for signs of corruption.

Hanoi, Capital City

Hanoi, Vietnam's capital city, was founded during the seventh century, when it was settled by members of China's Sui dynasty. From 1010 to 1802, Hanoi was the nation's capital, until Hue became the capital under French rule. It was again the capital of North Vietnam from 1954 until 1975, during the time Ho Chi Minh was president. When Vietnam was reunited, Hanoi became the nation's capital.

One of Hanoi's most well-known landmarks is the thousand-year-old One Pillar Pagoda (pictured). Though the French destroyed the pagoda in 1954, it was rebuilt by the Vietnamese government. Shaped like a lotus blossom, the Buddhist symbol of enlightenment, it is wooden and sits upon a stone pillar, meant to represent the stalk of a lotus flower.

Southwest of town is the Perfume Pagoda—Vietnam's most important Buddhist site. It is made up of several shrines carved into the limestone of the Huong Tich Mountains. It is the scene of an annual springtime pilgrimage, when thousands of Buddhists come to honor Quan Am, the goddess of compassion and mercy. During this time, the hills are filled with blossoms, giving the pagoda its name.

Population: 3.3 million

Year Founded: 1010 by King Ly Thai To

Altitude: 52 feet (15 m)

Average Daily Temperature: January, 62°F (17°C); July, 86°F (30°C)

Average Annual Rainfall: 66.2 inches (168 cm)

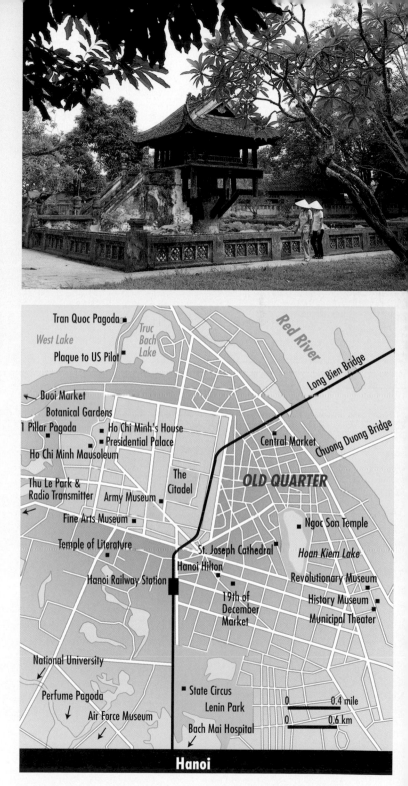

CHAPTER SIX

A Changing Economy

D OI MOI, "NEW CHANGE," IS THE KEY PHRASE TO DESCRIBE Vietnam's economy. It's the term for the program set in place by the government to strengthen Vietnam's lagging economy. Begun in 1986, it introduced several reforms to reduce government involvement in the economy and turn it over to private ownership. It has been a slow process, with plenty of problems along the way, but Vietnam keeps moving forward, making "new change."

A Bit of History

For centuries Vietnam was mainly a rural nation. Most people earned their living off the land. They grew crops and raised animals to feed their families. Depending on which foreign nation was in charge, farmers might have owned the land they lived on, or it might have been owned by the government, with the farmers paying to live on it. Some light industry, trade, and mining rounded out the economy. In the years just before the Vietnam War, the North Vietnamese government managed all

Opposite: **Vietnam's stock market opened in 2000.**

Agriculture is the cornerstone of Vietnam's economy.

business and industry, including farming. In the south, private investors managed most parts of the economy. The economy was stronger in the south than in the north.

In 1975, the government of the united Vietnam was in charge of business and industry. Production slowed. Government officials were not always good business leaders. Many products were poorly made, food was scarce, and income dropped. By 1986, it was obvious that change was needed. Doi moi has not been an immediate success, but it began the slow, gradual process of returning business and industry back to the citizens.

Agriculture

Agriculture has long been the cornerstone of Vietnam's economy. Along with forestry and fishing, it employs 71 percent of the nation's workers. Most farming takes place in the Mekong and Red River deltas, as well as other regions of the north and south. Central Vietnam is not good for agriculture because much of it is either mountainous or low-lying seacoast that is prone to regular damage from typhoons.

About 80 percent of all farmland is used to grow rice. Previously, the government owned the land—farmers worked for the government and were paid a set amount. But since 1990, most farmers hold long-term leases to the land they work. They have the right to use the land, but in return, they must pay the government a certain amount of their profits. They are free to use the remainder for their families. This leads the farmers to have a greater incentive to work harder.

Researchers work to improve rice crops.

This, along with improved farming techniques, has caused a dramatic increase in the annual harvests. Vietnam now grows enough rice to feed its citizens and to sell the extra to other parts of the world. In fact, only the United States and Thailand export more rice than Vietnam.

Other crops include sugarcane, peanuts, cassava, soybeans, corn, peppers, and sweet potatoes. Plantations growing fruits such as bananas, oranges, mangoes, pineapples, and coconuts are found in the Mekong River Delta.

Vietnam's Coffee Crop

Coffee production in the Central Highlands has made Vietnam the world's third-largest exporter of coffee, behind Colombia and Brazil. Only the petroleum, rice, textiles, and footwear industries earn more money in Vietnam. Coffee production has lifted many Central Highlands residents out of poverty.

French colonialists started coffee production in Vietnam during the 1920s. During the Vietnam War, the coffee industry faltered, like most of Vietnam's economy. The government tried to revive the crop following the war, but production didn't really take off until doi moi reforms took hold. In 1975, 40,000 acres (16,187 ha) were devoted to coffee production—today, there are more than 740,000 acres (299,467 ha).

Growth comes at a price. The vast amount of land that has been cleared for coffee production is depleting the nation's forests. In Dak Lak province where most of the coffee is grown, forests covered 70 percent of the land in 1975. Now, forests cover less than 15 percent. The land that is used for coffee growing isn't always used well. Farmers eager to quickly grow coffee use very strong fertilizers on the soil. It helps boost production for a few years, but it chemically alters the soil, destroying the nutrients that would be needed for future growth. This will make it difficult to produce as much coffee in the years to come. It remains to be seen whether Vietnam can maintain its coffee production.

Not all of Vietnam's crops are for consumption, though. Tobacco is grown here, along with jute for making rope. The silky fibers from Vietnam's kapok trees are used for insulation and for making life preservers and pillows. Mulberry bushes are grown for their leaves, which are fed to the silkworms that support silk production.

Some farmers raise shrimp in special ponds called *aquafarms*. Most of the nation's seafood, however, is caught in the sea by fishers. Lobster, squid, crab, and shrimp are all part of a growing export trade.

The forestry industry cuts down mostly original forestland, although some trees have been planted specifically for lumber. Some wood is used for the production of charcoal. Teak and mahogany are turned into furniture. Paper and pulp, lumber, plywood, and rattan products are also made from forest resources. In order to preserve forests, the government banned the export of timber in 1992.

Silkworms eating mulberry leaves

Fish for sale in a market

What Vietnam Grows, Makes, and Mines

Agriculture

Rice	31,394 metric tons
Corn	1,752 metric tons
Coffee	487 metric tons

Manufacturing

Cement	10,380 metric tons
Chemical fertilizers	1,120 metric tons
Rubber	215 metric tons

Mining

Crude petroleum	15,000 metric tons
Coal	9,097 metric tons
Salt	918 metric tons

Industry

Vietnam's industrial growth has come a long way in a very short time. When the French took over in the late 1800s, Vietnam had few factories. The French introduced some improvements to Vietnamese manufacturing, but the country suffered from shifting leadership and war for the next several decades. Not much changed until the war ended in 1975.

Most factories produce goods that Vietnamese people purchase. But more and more products are made for export as well, especially silk and other textiles, and such processed foods as seafood, coffee, tea, soft

Workers in a shoe factory

drinks, and condiments. Other items that are manufactured in Vietnam include paper goods, cement, chemical fertilizers, and footwear.

Resources

Since the late 1800s, heavy deposits of coal have been mined just outside Hanoi. This fuel is still mined today, and is one of Vietnam's major exports. Other important mineral resources include phosphates, tin, zinc, bauxite (used in the manufacture of aluminum), and manganese.

Oil and natural gas fields have been discovered just off Vietnam's coast in the South China Sea. Most companies

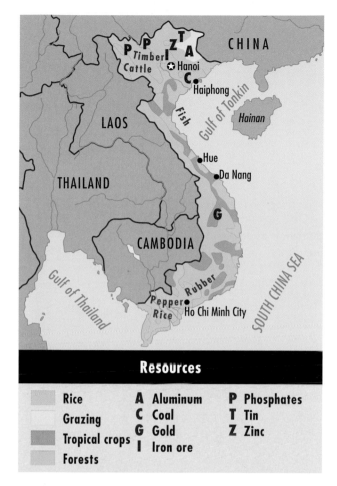

Resources

Rice	**A** Aluminum	**P** Phosphates
Grazing	**C** Coal	**T** Tin
Tropical crops	**G** Gold	**Z** Zinc
	I Iron ore	
Forests		

Women filling baskets at a coal mine

drilling for these resources are from foreign nations, but they pay for the rights to drill, and this money contributes to the Vietnamese economy.

Tourism

With its long, sandy coastline, towering mountains, forests and jungles, and interesting history, Vietnam might be a magnet for tourists. But its many attractive offerings have not always been

Tourism is a growing industry.

Currency and Finance

Vietnam's unit of currency is the *dong*. Currency comes in the form of bills—100, 200, 500, 1,000, 2,000, 5,000, 10,000, 20,000, and 50,000 notes. Because the largest bill, 50,000 dong, is worth less than U.S.$4, and because credit cards haven't caught on in most parts of the country, people carry a lot of bills with them. On the other hand, most things in Vietnam are not too expensive. A bowl of noodles and a cup of coffee from street vendors costs about 7,500 dong, or about 50 cents.

Banking services have improved in the country since the *doi moi* reforms. Before 1986, there was only one banking institution, which was run by the government. Since then, several more banks have opened, run both by local and international firms. The Vietnamese have better opportunities now for saving money and getting loans. Late in 2000, a small Vietnamese stock market opened.

publicized well. Lack of adequate transportation, lodging, food, and other comforts for tourists have kept visitors away. Vietnam has also suffered from its history—many people still believe it is a country ravaged by war and poverty. Vietnam has a lot to overcome. In recent years the country has worked hard and spent millions to promote tourism, and people are now making the trip. In the first six months of 1999 there were 860,000 visitors to Vietnam. This was a 7.5 percent increase over the number of tourists during the same period in 1998.

International Trade

Vietnam's main trading partners are Japan, Singapore, Thailand, and the United States, but it does business around

Vietnam does business around the world.

the world. Vietnam's main exports are rice, coal, forest products, wood, and rubber. Handicrafts, textiles, footwear, and processed foods are also exported. Vietnam imports machinery and motor vehicles.

Foreign investment in Vietnam grew rapidly for several years following doi moi, as outside businesses came to work on drilling for oil, building hotels, establishing banks, and opening factories. These businesses usually found that the reforms were working, but slowly. Many foreign business leaders have lost their early enthusiasm for Vietnam, as they find that the government is holding back on some of its doi moi promises. Foreign investment peaked at $8.6 billion in 1996. By 1999, it had dropped to $1.4 billion.

Doi Moi Today

Vietnam hasn't completely embraced capitalism. Many government leaders fear that capitalism is bringing in too much Western influence. Some government reforms progress slowly. Business dealings rarely move as smoothly as they do in other parts of the world. Most companies that were supposed to be turned over to private owners are still owned by the government. In 2000, only 450 of the more than 5,000 government-owned companies had been privatized.

The country is still poor, so sales of high-priced goods are low. More than half the population lives in poverty, particularly in rural areas. The average income throughout the country is about $350 per year, an amount that varies depending on the region. In Hanoi, where economic reforms have helped, the average annual income is about $1,000. In many rural areas, people live on about $50 a year.

Clearly, the doi moi reforms in Vietnam have gone a long way toward strengthening the economy, but there is still a long way to go.

The People and Their Language

VIETNAM IS THE THIRTEENTH MOST POPULOUS NATION IN the world with 76.3 million inhabitants. The average life expectancy is 66 years. Vietnam has faced overcrowding problems for nearly 600 years—today, with an average of more than 525 people for every square mile, it is one of the most densely populated countries in the world. Each year, the population increases by nearly 2 percent, but the government is trying to slow that rate by encouraging couples to have only one or two children.

Opposite: **Children on the central coast**

Population of Major Cities	
Ho Chi Minh City	5,200,000
Hanoi	3,300,000
Haiphong	1,500,000
Da Nang	375,000
Hue	265,000

The Vietnamese

The Vietnamese are descended from the Dong Son, the early inhabitants of the Ma River Valley in northern Vietnam. About 2,000 years ago, these people of Chinese and Indonesian origin mixed with others who had recently come to the Vietnam region from Thailand, Indonesia, and China. Together, they created the distinct Vietnamese people. Their numbers grew, and they fanned out southward along the central coast and into the Mekong River Delta. They lived near the water that was vital to growing rice. Today rice is still a staple, and the deltas of the Mekong and Red rivers are still the most populated areas in the country.

A Vietnamese family

A Chinese man in Cholon

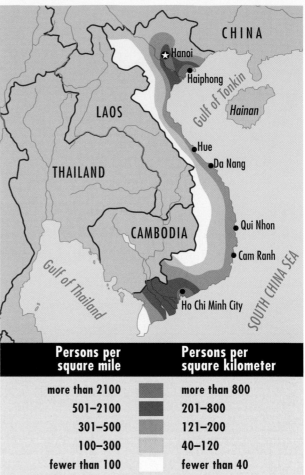

Persons per square mile		Persons per square kilometer
more than 2100		more than 800
501–2100		201–800
301–500		121–200
100–300		40–120
fewer than 100		fewer than 40

Ethnic Breakdown in National Population	
Vietnamese	84%
Chinese	2%
Sixty minorities	14%

Chinese

Only a few of the Chinese living in Vietnam consider themselves Chinese; most ethnic Chinese are known as *Hoas*. Still, they have the same ancestry—the Chinese who settled about 200 years ago in the Mekong Delta. Today most have moved into Vietnam's cities. Ho Chi Minh City's Cholon district has a large Chinese concentration, where many work as small business owners and retailers. Though most speak Vietnamese, many are also fluent in the Chinese dialect that was spoken in the region their ancestors came from.

While most Vietnamese people inhabited coastal regions, hill tribes took over the Central Highlands. Each of the tribes has its own customs and style of dress. In fact, their clothing is so distinctive that people who live in the region can usually tell which tribe a person belongs to according to what they are wearing.

The hill tribes living in the northern region are mostly farmers, growing such crops as tobacco, tea, fruit, and cotton. Many also raise pigs and poultry. The most remote of the northern hill tribes are the Hmong, who raise small farm animals as well as horses and cows. They grow fruits and vegetables.

Hmong tribespeople live in the north.

The Montagnards are a hill tribe living in the central and southern part of the country. They received their name from the French—it means "highlanders." The Montagnards came into contact with the French when they joined them and others in the fight against the Viet Minh.

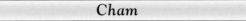

Cham

The Cham are another ethnic tribe that live near the Mekong Delta in the Phan Rang and the Phan Thiet regions. Their ancestors originated from Southeast Asian islands and founded Vietnam's first kingdom, Champa, on the coast. Indian explorers came to this area later and influenced the

Cham dancers and musicians performing

culture. Even today, the women often wear a piece of silk draped around them, similar to the sari worn by women in India. They often wear their long hair tied up on their head, and perfume themselves with musk and camphor scents, as do Indian women.

Language

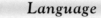

The country's official language is Vietnamese, also known as *kinh*. Though each ethnic minority has its own language, most also speak Vietnamese. It is this common language that bonds the people together as a nation.

People who study language are unsure as to the exact origins of the language, but agree that it shows a variety of influences. The Thai, southern Chinese, and Mon-Khmer speaking settlers all contributed to the language, as did Malaysians and Polynesians.

Classical Chinese language, though, had the greatest impact on the Vietnamese language. During the 1,000 years of Chinese rule, Mandarin was the official language of the government, arts, and education. While traditional Vietnamese was still spoken, its meanings and pronunciations were influenced by the Chinese language. Vietnam's written script, too, began to follow the style of Chinese characters. This Vietnamese character system, known as *chu nom*, was popular in literature until about 100 years ago.

Roman letters, similar to the English alphabet, were introduced in the 1600s by Catholic missionaries from France, Spain, Italy, and Portugal. They wanted to spread their message about God through a written language, and devised a writing system that could be transcribed and written down in the Vietnamese language. This system, called *quoc ngu*, caught on throughout the land at the end of the nineteenth century and eventually replaced chu nom. Quoc ngu grew in popularity during the 1920s and 1930s, when scholars wrote many books on social and political issues that were widely read among middle-class Vietnamese. During this period, though, quoc ngu was still unfamiliar to Vietnam's poorest citizens. They simply had to spend all their daylight hours working to feed themselves, and had no time or opportunity for education. It wasn't until 1945, when the government made primary education

Learning to write

mandatory, that literacy become common for these people. Today, more than 90 percent of all Vietnamese read quoc ngu.

Quoc ngu requires additional markings on the letters to indicate which way the word is meant to be pronounced. These are called diacritical marks. They are important because different pronunciations of the same word can have greatly different meanings. There are six different tones signified by the diacritical marks. A common example is the word *ma*. It can mean tomb, ghost, but, mother, rice seedling, or horse, depending upon how it is spoken.

Once, a U.S. general, hoping to impress a local crowd, tried to tell them in their own language: "I am honored to be here." His words may have been right, but the tone was all wrong. What the Vietnamese people heard was, "The sunburned duck lies sleeping."

Most people in Vietnam read quoc ngu.

Quoc Ngu

Quoc ngu is the written form of the Vietnamese language. It has the same twenty-six letters of the alphabet in its language as does English, but accent marks, called diacritical marks, are added to some of the letters to show the way the letter is to be pronounced. So there are actually more letter sounds than in English. There are twenty-seven consonants and twelve vowels in quoc ngu. The consonants are generally pronounced the same way as they are pronounced in English, but with a few exceptions. For example, "gi" sounds like "y" in English, while the English "ch" sound is spelled "tr" in quoc ngu.

Body Language

Among English speakers, different tones of voice are often used to indicate emotions. Because Vietnamese speakers use different tones of voice to mean different words, emotions must be shown through posture and gestures. It is considered impolite, especially for women and girls, to look a stranger directly in the eyes when speaking. Most Vietnamese will look away when speaking to a new person. In Vietnam, it is a symbol of aggression to cross your arms or put your hands on your hips, so this is rarely done. It is also impolite to point your finger or to point your foot at someone when your legs are crossed. This is a way of showing your feelings of superiority over the person to whom you're pointing.

Names

Names in Vietnam are used opposite of the way North Americans use names. In Vietnam, the family name, or the last name, comes first. The middle name is second—usually all members of a certain generation in a family have the same middle name. Individual names come last. Names often have a special meaning in the Vietnamese language—many parents believe the names they give their children will impact them for life. Boys' names usually represent some virtue or character trait the parents wish for their son, while girls' names are often those of beautiful things, such as flowers or birds.

Family Names

The most common family name in Vietnam is *Nguyen*, pronounced like "win." Nearly half the population has this name, which dates back to the period of the Nguyen dynasty, 1802–1954. This ruling family allowed citizens to take on their name. There are about 300 family names throughout Vietnam.

Vietnamese boys

A Patchwork
of Beliefs

90

RELIGION IS SOMETHING LIKE A PATCHWORK QUILT TO many people in Vietnam. They take traditions of one faith and customs of another, add teachings from great leaders, then arrange them in a pattern that suits their personal needs. It is a mix of faiths that has evolved over centuries.

Vietnam's constitution gives all its citizens religious freedom, although there are some restrictions. Religious practices may not break other laws, they may not prevent anyone from doing useful work, and they cannot put the security of the country in danger. Most Vietnamese people are Buddhists, but there are also Catholics and a small number of people following

Opposite: **Lighting incense at a shrine**

Buddhists worshiping in a pagoda

Religions in Vietnam	
Buddhist	67%
Catholic	8%
Cao Dai	3%
Hoa Hao	2%
Protestant	1%
Other	19%

religions native to Vietnam, as well as Protestants, Taoists, Confucianists, Hindus, and Muslims. It is difficult to give a number to people in any religion in this country, where religious lines are not clearly drawn.

Buddhism

The most common religion in Vietnam—followed by about two-thirds of the population—is Buddhism. Buddhists strive to become enlightened, that is, completely understanding life and their place in it. They try to live nonviolently and with compassion, in a way that frees them from wanting material things.

Buddhist monks begging for alms

Buddhist monks and nuns in Vietnam are strict vegetarians. These vegans do not eat any meat, fish, or animal by-products, such as eggs and dairy products. They believe that all living things have souls. Other Buddhists in Vietnam do not always follow such a strict diet—for example, many will eat fish sauce with their meals. During religious holidays, however, nearly all Buddhists obey the strict dietary rules.

Four Noble Truths of Buddhism

There are "Four Noble Truths" that the Buddhist faith is based upon. These are that people are born to suffer during life; suffering is caused by the desire for pleasure and possessions; suffering ends when people give up their attachments to all things, including themselves; the way to end this attachment is to follow the eight-fold path of right understanding, right thought, right speech, right action, right livelihood, right effort, right mindfulness, and right concentration. Following these truths could lead to a state of bliss.

Buddhism has several forms, but two are most common in Vietnam. Traders coming from India through Burma and Thailand introduced Theravada Buddhism into southern Vietnam. There are about 400,000 followers, mostly among the Khmer people of the Mekong region. About one hundred years later, Chinese people introduced Mahayana Buddhism in northern Vietnam. This is the form most Vietnamese follow.

Buddha

Buddhists are followers of Buddha, who was born Siddhartha Gautama during the sixth century B.C. in the country that is now Nepal. Buddha means "the enlightened one." His family was wealthy, but he gave up wealth to pursue a life that would be free of suffering. He spent many years in contemplation and finally achieved a state of bliss known as *nirvana*. He devoted the rest of his life to teaching Buddhism's Noble Truths to others.

Buddhist Pagodas

Called *Chi* by the Vietnamese, Buddhist pagodas are found throughout the nation. Most pagodas were built during the eighteenth and nineteenth centuries as temples. They are still in use. Though each pagoda features unique characteristics, most have several elements in common. A bell tower is typical, and most have a walled courtyard where there are ponds and religious statues, helping believers to contemplate such values as compassion and charity.

There is a main hall in every pagoda where the public is welcome. Beyond that are smaller rooms, usually on a slightly higher level. Altars and prayer tables are here for more serious worship. There is usually one altar dedicated to deceased Buddhist monks and nuns, for example.

Statues are an important part of all pagodas. Each pagoda features two large statues representing the guardians of Buddhist law. These are "Mister Charitable," shown with a white face and holding a pearl, and "Mister Wicked," who has a red face. Mr. Charitable sees everything, while his partner passes out justice on the world.

The top row of statues on the main altars represents the three forms of Buddha of the highest level—the Historical Buddha, the Present Buddha, and the Future Buddha. More rows feature other Buddhas. Among them may be the all-powerful Buddha of a thousand arms and eyes, the laughing Buddha who grants wishes, and the Nine Dragon Buddha, most common in pagodas of northern Vietnam.

A major difference between the two is that the Mahayana Buddhists believe that some people are *bodhisattvas*. These people have reached nirvana, but chose to remain on earth to help others reach salvation. This belief was popular among Vietnamese when the religion was introduced, because they already had a whole array of local saints and spirits that they could incorporate into the religion by considering them as bodhisattvas. This acceptance allowed them to take up the new religion, while still maintaining their old beliefs. In fact, most Vietnamese Buddhists' actual beliefs and practices include a mix of many other religions as well.

Catholic priests outside a cathedral

Christianity

Christian religions were first brought to Vietnam by Portuguese and Spanish missionaries who came to the nation's northern coast during the 1500s. In the next century, permanent missions were established by Catholic Jesuits.

In its first several centuries in Vietnam, Christianity's popularity rose and fell. At times, particularly enthusiastic missionaries could get thousands of people to convert. But such times would be followed by periods of revolt against Christianity, which teaches several principles opposed to Vietnamese culture. In particular,

Christianity disapproves of ancestor worship and a variety of gods. It also teaches that all people are equal, in contrast to Confucianism.

Because their faith often went against Vietnamese tradition, Christians were persecuted in the 1800s, and many were put to death. During French rule, Catholicism became strong. Today, there are about 6 million Catholics in Vietnam. Several hundred thousand more fled the country in the mid-1970s following the communist takeover of Vietnam, afraid of persecution if they remained.

There is also a small number of Christians of Protestant faiths. *Tin Lanh* is the Vietnamese name for the Good News, a Protestant faith with about 400,000 members.

A Tin Lanh church

Symbol of Cao Dai

Cao Dai and Hoa Hao

Vietnam is the birthplace of two faiths that formed in the early 1900s: Cao Dai and Hoa Hao. Cao Dai has about 2 million followers, mostly in southern Vietnam. Ngo Van Chieu founded the religion over a period of several years. At its head is the Supreme Being, known as *Cao Dai*, or "High Place," represented by the symbol of an all-seeing eye shown on a blue

Cao Dai priests stand by a painting honoring saints from Chinese and French cultures

globe. Followers believe the Cao Dai has been known to the world in several human forms, including Buddha, Jesus Christ, and other religious leaders. They celebrate such holidays as the days of Taoism and Confucianism; Christmas, the birth of Christ; and Buddha's birthday. They also honor many saints, holy people, and heroes of more modern times: Napoleon Bonaparte, Joan of Arc, Louis Pasteur, William Shakespeare, and Winston Churchill. Local heroes are saints as well.

Hoa Hao is a very simple, pure form of Buddhism. Founder Huynh Phu envisioned a religion in which followers find their direct path to God through prayer, reflection, and fasting. Most of Hoa Hao's 1.5 million followers today live in the Mekong Delta region.

Confucianism

Confucianism is not really a religion, but a set of principles and values that followers use to guide their lives. It was based on the teaching of K'ung Fu-tzu, a name later Latinized into Confucius. He was born into a wealthy Chinese family in 551 B.C., and became a court official. After observing the political and legal process, and forming ideas about the nature of power and government, he spent twenty years traveling around China. He spoke about the need for social and political reform, hoping to bring about peace in a way that would benefit both the government and individuals.

Confucius's teachings centered on the importance of correct behavior, solid education, and loyal service. He endorsed such traits as mercy, respectfulness, sincerity, nonviolence, kindness, and selflessness.

Confucius

Though he said little about spiritual beliefs, he emphasized the need to provide offerings to ancestors and spirits.

When Confucious observed the natural world, he saw that forms of life were arranged hierarchically, that is, they are classified according to rank. People, he believed, should be classified in a similar manner, with hierarchies based on class, profession, and gender. People of high class and important professions held top rankings.

Confucius felt strongly that leaders should rule over their subjects through the power of good example, rather than force. They were expected to treat their citizens as their own children, and in turn, citizens were to be obedient. This is one of the reasons the Chinese were eager to introduce

Confucianism to their Vietnamese subjects when they ruled the country. They felt it was a good way to control people and keep them peaceful. Still, this teaching implied that revolt was acceptable if leaders did not treat their subjects well. Eventually, the Vietnamese people took this to heart in their rebellion against their Chinese oppressors.

Even though Chinese rule is long past, many Vietnamese still follow Confucian guidelines. The respect shown to most teachers, religious leaders, and political officials is just one example of this.

Lao-tzu

Taoism

Taosim is a religion based on a book written by Lao-tzu, the "Old Master," in China during the sixth century B.C. His book, *Tao-te Ching*, or Book of the Way, stressed a belief in the spirit world. "Tao," is based on spontaneity and intuition, is invisible, and cannot be taught. All creation, even that which is eternal, springs from it. Though the Tao cannot be explained with words, followers believe that it is possible to achieve what is known as ultimate stillness through compassionate and nonviolent behavior on earth, combined with a personal spiritual quest.

One of the central principles of Taoism is the belief in the balance of the universe—the idea that everything in nature is complimented by an opposite. This is known as *yin* and *yang*, or male and female principles. One example is the sun, which is yang, or male. It is balanced by the earth, which is yin, female. The balance between the two is harmony. Tao is the experience of that harmony. It is important that humans do not disrupt the balance in nature. Followers worship many gods, as well as saints and the spirits of those who had lived on earth before them.

Taoism was brought to Vietnam during the long period of Chinese rule. For several centuries it was as popular as Confucianism. By the 1400s Taoism began to decline, and today few people follow it strictly. Taoism still exists in Vietnam, though, both as a folk religion in some regions, and as a part of the range of beliefs followed by many people.

Tam Giao

Tam Giao, or the Triple Religion, is a practice followed by many Vietnamese Buddhists. Buddhist principles are combined with Confucian ancestor worship and the worship of Taoist gods. This idea of accepting other religious beliefs is allowed by all three religions and philosophies.

In keeping with Tam Giao, most Vietnamese temples contain items from all three beliefs. There are statues of the major Buddhas and many other Buddhas, as well as statues of such Taoist gods as *Ngoc Hoang*, the Jade Emperor. A side altar will often hold photos of deceased relatives of people from the

A small altar hanging from a tree

community. A person visiting the temple will often pray to several gods or burn incense as an offering to the spirits of the gods and ancestors.

Many Vietnamese families also provide an area in their homes for a small altar. Here they worship and honor their dead relatives. Even those who aren't particularly religious usually follow this practice. Often pictures or other reminders of these people are placed nearby. The Vietnamese believe that their ancestors can bring their families good fortune, but they must honor the dead by performing small ceremonies and paying respect. Sometimes they place food at the altar to share with their ancestors, and small amounts of paper money may be burnt as an offering. If these rituals are not performed, they believe the ancestors may become angry and cause problems for the living.

Animism

The belief that many things in nature, such as trees, rivers, and clouds, have souls is known as *animism*. This is the general term given to a whole host of primitive religions followed by tribes living in Vietnam's Central Highlands. A key element of animism is a belief that the universe is divided into three parts: the sky, earth, and humans. All are ruled over by *Ong Troi*, Lord of the Heavens. He is assisted by the spirits found throughout nature. The natural spirits with special powers are the dragon, symbolizing power and intelligence; the phoenix (a bird rising from ashes) representing beauty and peace; the turtle, representing a long life; and the kylin, a creature similar to a unicorn, symbolizing wisdom.

People must be careful not to use the name of a spirit, because that would call the spirit down upon the speaker and bring him or her bad fortune. Particularly dangerous are the spirits of such animals as crocodiles, elephants, and tigers—believers are careful not to call these creatures by their names.

Most Central Highland villages also honor a guardian spirit. This spirit may be a legendary god, or it may be the spirit of a great local or national hero.

Other Religions

Other religions, such as Islam and Hinduism, are practiced in Vietnam as well, though by relatively few people. One of the interesting things about religion in Vietnam is that while spirituality is important in the lives of most Vietnamese, strong loyalty to one particular religion is not. Instead, people adapt and blend religions to suit their own needs.

Arts and Culture of Vietnam

MUSIC IS AN IMPORTANT ASPECT OF MUCH OF VIETnam's culture. The world's oldest-known musical instruments are found in Vietnam. Even the Vietnamese language can be considered music for its dependence on notes and tones. It is a language often expressed in poetry. Vietnam is the birthplace of an unusual form of puppetry performed in water. Vietnam's culture is rich with music and tradition.

Opposite: **Puppeteers at a water puppet performance**

Playing a dan da stone lithophone

Music

Gongs are the most common musical instruments in Vietnam, though they exist in many forms, including xylophones and drums. In fact, the world's oldest-known instrument hails from Vietnam's Central Highlands. Known as the *dan da* stone lithophone, it is something like a stone-age xylophone. A slate quarry in the region produces special rock with a nice ringing tone. A set of six or more rocks, in varying sizes, along with a wooden mallet for hitting them, comprise the dan da.

Coin clappers are another distinctive Vietnamese gong, consisting of a rattle made from old coins, struck by an attached wooden clapper. Hollow bamboo stalks are used to make flutes and similar wind instruments. Bamboo

stalks are also used in gong-type instruments—different lengths of bamboo produce different sounds when struck.

Many of these instruments are used in the folk music that originated in the Central Highlands of the country. Today, many of these songs are played by large orchestras using instruments brought in from the West. This entertainment, popular in the cities, is known as modernized folk music. Traditional musicians are glad for the wider audience attracted by the folk music, but most people are not pleased that orchestras play music that they feel belongs to them.

Vietnam has few popular singing stars. The music industry in the country is not well established enough to promote performers. But that doesn't mean there aren't any singers. On the contrary, the country is full of people who love to sing, and there are many performers who are quite popular at local levels. Karaoke, in which anybody can take the stage and sing, is a popular leisure activity.

Phung Thao is one famous young singer. The daughter of an American

Costumed musicians performing with traditional instruments

Trinh Cong Son

Trinh Cong Son, who died in April 2001, was one of Vietnam's few popular singing stars, probably the most famous. He was born in 1939, but his popularity dates back to the Vietnam War. He wrote several songs while in hiding, avoiding the military draft. His antiwar lyrics were so controversial that his songs were banned by the South Vietnamese government. However, his tunes were so catchy, and the lyrics so well written, that many people sang along with his songs anyway. More than 2 million copies of his 1969 album *Lullaby*, were sold in Japan. Following the war the new government sent him to a labor camp for four years. He continued writing songs, more than 600, throughout his life.

serviceman and a Vietnamese woman, she says that she was picked on as a child because of her mixed heritage. Today, her songs are a blend of traditional Vietnamese and modern American music.

Theater

Vietnam has a long history of theater, but because much of the dialogue is sung rather than spoken, the performances are often more similar to opera than drama. The two oldest forms are *Hat Cheo* and *Hat Truong*, while a more modern form is *Hat Cai Luong*.

Hat Cheo is at least 1,000 years old. Begun in the Red River Delta, it's a staging of well-known legends and common events set to tunes. The audience usually knows the plot, but the actors have some leeway about how they wish to interpret and express the story. Audience members beat drums to show their approval. Hat Truong, introduced by the Chinese about 800 years ago, was first presented for royalty. The stories are mostly epic historic tales, such as the importance of the relationship

A Hat Cai Luong actor applying stage makeup

between a king and his subjects, highlighting principles of Confucianism.

"Renovated theater" is the English term for Hat Cai Luong, drama that originated less than 100 years ago in Vietnam's Mekong region. Heavily influenced by the French, it contains spoken parts and contemporary themes. Modern instruments, such as keyboards and electric guitars, provide most of the music. Though most people prefer Hat Cai Luong, all three of Vietnam's theater forms are losing popularity. People are more interested in television and videos these days.

Water Puppetry

While traditional theater may be less popular in Vietnam, another traditional form of performance is becoming more popular. Water puppet shows are unique to Vietnam and very entertaining.

Called *roi nouc*, these shows are performed by puppeteers who stand knee-deep in water, hidden from the audience by bamboo screens. The large puppets—lions, ducks, unicorns, dragons, and more—appear to be walking in water themselves. The puppets are often elaborate, able to blow smoke or throw balls. Special effects include fireworks that add excitement to the shows. The performances usually portray folktales from Vietnam's history.

The Golden Turtle

"The Golden Turtle and the Lake of the Restored Sword" is one of the most famous water puppet shows, based on a tale about Hoan Kiem Lake, located in the middle of Hanoi. The story revolves around Le Loi, a great Vietnamese hero who fought successfully against the Chinese. According to legend, he was fishing on the lake one day, pulled in his net, and discovered a powerful, gleaming sword. Ten years later, after being named king, he returned to thank the lake. While he was in a boat on the lake, the sword flew out from its holder and was seized by a golden turtle. Quickly, the turtle disappeared under the water.

Since then, the lake has been called the Lake of the Restored Sword. Today, Tortoise Tower, a three-tiered pavilion (pictured), sits on a small island in the middle of the lake. It is a monument to the story and an important symbol of Hanoi.

The techniques behind water puppetry were kept secret for centuries, only passed down from older to younger men within families. Women were not allowed to learn, for fear they would spread secrets to their husbands' families. Because of this secrecy, water puppetry was quickly becoming a dying art. In 1984, a French cultural organization revived it. Today, several troupes tour Vietnam to perform water puppet shows.

Poetry and Literature

Poetry is the most beloved and traditional form of literature in Vietnam, handed down from generation to generation. Many Vietnamese people know one particular poem by heart, *Kim Van Kieu* (The Tale of Kieu) by Nguyen Du. In the poem, a young girl struggles against many hardships to maintain her family's honor. Other poems often deal with warfare. They describe the love of country and the willingness to fight for it against foreign intruders.

Not only do the Vietnamese enjoy poetry written by others, but many write poetry themselves. They share it in courtship, or use it as a way to encourage themselves or others who are facing such hardships as poverty, illness, or fear.

Written literature, meant to be read silently, has never been as popular in Vietnam as poetry. The main themes of Vietnamese literature echo those of its poetry—love of nation and bravery.

Arts

There is not much in the way of painting to be found in Vietnam, at least not the kind of painting on canvas produced in many other cultures. It never really caught on in Vietnam. But there are artists nonetheless. One beautiful art form found in Vietnam is lacquerware: dishes, small boxes, and other objects are finished with a deep sheen of red or black and often decorated with other colors as well. This art form is practiced throughout Asia. Vietnamese lacquerware is of very high quality.

Block prints are another popular craft in Vietnam. Usually these prints show scenes of peace and cheerfulness. The designs are carved into wood, covered with ink, and pressed onto paper. These are popular to give as gifts during the Tet holiday.

Lacquerware

In rural areas, particularly in the Highlands, people weave fabrics to make clothing and blankets. Bamboo and other grasses are woven into baskets, mats, and siding for homes. Though these are common, everyday items created for a useful purpose, the skill and beauty in the weaving raises them to the level of art.

Detail of French colonial architecture in Hanoi

Architecture

Throughout the nation's history, no uniquely Vietnamese architecture ever really developed. Instead, there are two forms of architecture commonly seen throughout the country, resulting from periods when Vietnam was controlled by the French and Chinese. Many of Vietnam's most distinctive buildings follow one of these forms.

This unusual mix of architecture is particularly obvious in Hanoi. It was filled with temples and pagodas, buildings with architecture heavily influenced by the long Chinese domination of the country. The French who occupied the city, beginning in 1883, tore down many of these buildings and replaced them with buildings in classic ornate French style, on broad streets, as was common in France. Today, the two styles stand side by side throughout the city, a combination that is a silent testimony to Hanoi's history.

Boys playing soccer in Hue

Sports

Soccer is one of the most popular sports in Vietnam, just as it is in many parts of the world. Young people throughout the country play the game. Another popular sport is swimming, particularly among those living near the sea, since there are beautiful beaches in the central and southern portions of the country. Tennis, volleyball, and badminton are common pastimes. Bicycling is also very common, though it is more a necessary means of transportation than it is a form of recreation.

Professional sports, though, are not well established. Most Vietnamese view sports as a social, friendly event, not as a competitive spectator show, so there are few professional athletes. But individual athletics are encouraged—many young people learn such martial arts as judo, tae kwon do, and karate.

Vietnam's First Olympic Medal

Vietnam won its first Olympic medal during the 2000 Summer Olympics in Sydney, Australia. Tran Hieu Ngan (on left) won a silver medal in the women's featherweight class of tae kwon do. A twenty-six-year-old from the small fishing village of Tuy Hoa on the central coast, she began learning tae kwon do when she was fourteen, and become the national champion when she was twenty.

This was the first time tae kwon do was an Olympic sport. It is an ancient martial art, focusing on kicks with bare feet.

Holidays and Celebrations

Tet Nguyen Dan is Vietnam's most important holiday. It is a weeklong New Year celebration held in late January that also marks the start of spring. Families pray for good luck and blessings for the new year. There are elaborate, colorful parades and games. People spend time with relatives and friends and exchange gifts. Different traditions of the holiday developed in different parts of the country. Flower shows are popular during Tet in some regions,

Dragon dancing in a Tet parade

Arts and Culture of Vietnam   **113**

others celebrate with loud firecrackers. Many children enjoy *hat doi*, a fun time where groups of children sing to each other.

Many other festivals vary from village to village. The Hmong tribes of the Central Highlands celebrate their New Year with a monthlong festival in spring. There is plenty of good food. Families clean and decorate their homes together, then gather for firecrackers, games, music, and dancing. In Thi Cam village, near Hanoi, a rice-cooking festival takes place

Children perform a traditional dance during the spring festival.

Birth and Marriage Customs

When a baby is born in Vietnam, it is unlikely that the father would be present. The mother is usually tended by adult female members of her family. When the baby is born, it is considered to already be one year old.

Most Vietnamese people don't celebrate birthdays. Instead, people add another year to their age during Tet. Only the first anniversary of a person's birth is sometimes celebrated. The ceremony, known as *thoi noi*, symbolizes the child leaving the cradle. The young child sits in the middle of a room, and parents put items around the baby representing different careers the child may eventually choose. It is believed that whichever item the child touches first foretells his or her future.

Traditionally, children usually remained with their families until they were married, then the couple lived with the groom's family. Often, parents arranged weddings for the bride and groom, and the couple had little contact prior to their marriage. But all these practices are becoming rare. In urban areas, many young, single people live away from their families, and married couples have their own apartments. Dating is common and similar to dating customs in North America. Most people want to choose their own mates, though it's important that the family accept him or her. Divorce is still uncommon, and considered shameful, though divorce rates are rising in Vietnam.

each January 8. Teams fetch water, make a fire, and cook rice. Taste-testers select the winner and award prizes.

Other local festivals concern the farming season, highlighting the desire for fair weather and good crops. These are often times when the strict guidelines of proper behavior under Confucianism are relaxed. People are free to celebrate joyously and forget for a little while the difficulties of normal life.

TEN

Daily Life in Vietnam

A family meal

VIETNAMESE STYLE HAS BORROWED FROM MANY SOURCES— from the French and Chinese during their centuries of control, from the various religions and philosophies that are central to their lives, and from the West, with its economic style moving in. The Vietnamese have taken all these influences, combined them with their centuries of history, and blended them into a way of life that is distinctly Vietnamese.

Food

The most usual element of many Vietnamese meals is rice. It is served with foods both sweet and savory, mixed with small amounts of other foods. When the family eats, each person takes some rice from a common bowl into his or her own bowl, and then covers it with the fruits, vegetables, or meats that accompany the meal.

Opposite: **Many people use bicycles and motor scooters to get around.**

King Hung and Banh Chung

Banh chung is a delicious sticky-rice cake, famous throughout Vietnam and enjoyed every Tet as a celebration of the new year. To many Vietnamese, the Tet celebration wouldn't be complete without it. The cake is a thick square of sweetened sticky-rice, which is rice that has been cooked in sweet coconut milk. It's filled with mung beans and peppery pork, then wrapped in a banana leaf and boiled. According to legend, banh chung was created in honor of King Hung of the Hung dynasty. To celebrate the new year, he asked for a gift from each of his children. His third child was poor, and couldn't afford fancy gifts, but she created this special treat for him. The king was very pleased. He decreed that banh chung should be eaten every new year, and so it has been for two thousand years.

Noodles are another major element of Vietnamese meals. Hot noodle soup, called *pho*, is very popular for breakfast; it is made with flavored broth, silky thin noodles, and sometimes a bit of meat. The day's largest meal is eaten at noon, when workers take a long break to avoid being out during the greatest heat.

Fish is Vietnam's most common meat. It's especially popular in the south, where lighter foods are usual during the warmer periods. But fish can be purchased throughout the country—anyone can fish and sell the catch. The sea, rivers, and rice paddies all provide a place to fish, but many dig ponds in which to raise catfish, carp, and shellfish. No part of the fish goes to waste. Even the head is enjoyed—it's prized for its flavor and is supposed to bring good luck to those who eat it.

Pork, beef, and poultry are a small part of the Vietnamese diet, because they are too expensive for most people to eat regularly. These meats are just for special occasions. Some other meats eaten include bat, dog, cobra, frogs, and eel. Eggs are another source of protein. Little goes to waste—duck tongues are considered to be a delicacy.

Vegetables used in Vietnamese cooking include cucumber, carrots, and daikon, which is a Japanese radish. But the most popular vegetable is *rau muong* (water spinach). Most Vietnamese eat this every day. Its leaves are soft and wilted

Nuoc Mam

What salt is to American cooking, what soy sauce is to Chinese food, *nuoc mam* is to Vietnamese cuisine. It's the must-have condiment—most meals would not be considered complete without it. Nuoc mam is a fermented fish sauce that was at one time usually homemade, but now most Vietnamese buy it already prepared.

Here's how it's made. Small silvery fish, a certain type of anchovies called *ca com*, are packed into large wooden barrels, along with several layers of salt. Then they are left to ferment. After about three months, the "juice" that has gathered at the bottom of the barrel is tapped out, and poured back over the top. The mixture then sits for six months longer. When the juice is drained off again, it is ready. Some people use it just like that, others mix it with hot peppers, garlic, lime juice, or other flavorings. The bottle usually sits on the table for all meals, ready to add just the right flavor to the food.

Vietnamese Holidays

Tet	Sometime in January or February, depending upon lunar calendar.
New Year's Day	January 1
Vietnam Day	January 27
Anniversary of the Founding of the Vietnamese Communist Party	February 3
Liberation Day	April 30
International Workers Day, or May Day	May 1
Vesak, Buddha's birthday	First full moon in May
Anniversary of Dien Bien Phu 1954 victory	May 7
Ho Chi Minh's birthday	May 19
National Day	September 2
Buddha's Enlightenment	December 8
Christmas Day	December 25

when cooked, but the stems stay crunchy. It's used in soups and stir-fries. Onions are popular, along with soybeans and bamboo shoots, sweet potatoes, and sugarcane. Manioc is a starchy root vegetable similar to a potato. Corn on the cob is a favorite. Many vegetables are often grown in small gardens near each home.

Vietnamese diets include a variety of fruits. *Vu sua* is a fruit called a milk apple and pomelo is a type of grapefruit. Other fruits include *chom chom* and the sweet, juicy *rambutan*. Vietnamese also enjoy mangoes, bananas, coconuts, and mangosteens—a sweet and juicy fruit with a hard rind.

Most people purchase only a little food at a time, just enough for the next meal or two, since few own refrigerators,

especially in rural areas. They purchase their food from street vendors. Vendors set up small stalls along the road and often sell foods they've grown themselves. Other street vendors sell prepared food, usually bowls of hot soup, small dumplings, rice cakes, meatballs, or candy. Vietnamese typically enjoy snacking throughout the day, so these food vendors are popular.

A street vendor selling prepared food

Top left: **This city family wears typical Western clothing.**

Top right: **Girls wearing ao dai**

Clothing

Typical Western clothing, similar to what most Americans wear, is most common in Vietnam. But traditional clothes are seen, too. Many Vietnamese women wear the traditional *ao dai*, a long dress slit up the side, with a loose-fitting pair of slacks underneath. The traditional formal outfit for men is called an *ao the*, a long gown with a slit on the side, usually in brown or black. For casual times, men traditionally wear a brown shirt with white pants. Rural people usually go barefoot or wear simple sandals. In cities, wooden sandals or Western-style clothing and shoes are common.

Hats are important protection from the hot sun. People who work outdoors are often seen in the traditional cone-shaped hats called *non la*. These are made from woven palm leaves.

Homes

Rural homes in Vietnam are often made from woven bamboo siding, held in place by wooden beams. Roofs made of tightly bound grass keep the rain out. There are some regional differences, though, depending upon the climate. Tile roofs are more common in the chillier northern areas. It's becoming more common to see sturdier roofs these days, made of sheet metal or plastic.

A traditional rural home

Some city-dwellers live in large apartment buildings.

In cities, homes are more modern, with a few small rooms, bathroom, and kitchen. There is often a small yard where children can play, but it is also used for outdoor cooking and laundry. Most city dwellers live in apartments or in houses made from wood and woven mats. Brick and tile are often used.

Education

Confucianism places great value on learning, and Vietnam's educational system shows that the country takes this seriously. Primary and secondary schooling are free to Vietnamese children, and children ages five to eleven must attend classes.

Vietnam is a highly literate nation—94 percent of Vietnamese can read and write. Many learn a foreign language as well.

Students often wear simple uniforms to school—dark slacks, white shirts, and a scarf. Classes typically run all year long, six days a week, four hours a day. Children begin their elementary schooling at age five, learning basic subjects for five years. Then they attend a secondary school for four years. In addition to history and geography, a foreign language is required. Most students choose English, although French, Japanese, Russian, and Mandarin Chinese are options.

Schoolchildren in Hanoi

Students who pass an examination after four years may go directly to work, to a vocational school to learn a specific skill, or to high school to continue their education. Many students who do well in high school and vocational school then choose to enter a university. The country has five major universities located in Ho Chi Minh City, Hanoi, Hue, Da Nang, and Thai Nguyen, and more than forty colleges and technical schools. Science and technology classes are especially stressed, but the country's lack of high-tech equipment makes it difficult to study these areas. Many students go abroad for their college education, often to Japan or the United States.

Transportation

Though there are thousands of miles of roads in Vietnam, most people don't own cars. Bikes and motor scooters are the most popular methods of getting around. Many people simply walk, or hitch a ride on a water buffalo from time to time in the rural areas. Those who want to take it easy can get a ride on a *cyclo*—a three-wheeled carriage pushed from behind by a pedaling driver. These are also sometimes known as pedicabs or trishaws—in Vietnamese they are called *xich-lo*.

Getting from northern Vietnam to southern Vietnam can be difficult. Because of the hilly terrain that makes up most of the center of the country, the transportation routes are limited to the thin coastal strip of land. One major highway and a railway travel through this area, connecting Ho Chi Minh City and Hanoi. The government is currently building a second highway to link these two main cities.

Roller-skating in Ho Chi Minh City

Free Time

Children in Vietnam spend their free time the way most kids do—playing with their friends. They like to jump rope, pretend they are grownups, or play soccer and other games. Most families that can afford a television have one, and really like to watch it. Others visit friends who have television sets. A trip to the zoo is a popular family outing, and movies are fun, too. Adults living in the city enjoy karaoke lounges. In rural areas, such games as chess and card games fill leisure time.

The Future

What will the future hold for Vietnam and its people? With the doi moi reforms, and a growing openness to trade with the rest of the world, it seems likely that the nation will become more prosperous. Still, many traditional values will probably remain unchanged. As they have for centuries, most Vietnamese people will continue to hold great respect for their ancestors, love for their families, and pride in their nation.

Timeline

Vietnamese History

Dong Son culture is established.	3000 B.C.
Chinese conquer the northern part of what is now Vietnam and begin the spread of their cultural influence.	111 B.C.
Trung sisters lead successful revolt against China and begin three years of rule.	A.D. 40
Chinese rule in Vietnam is ended. Vietnam becomes an independent state.	938
The Ly dynasty controls Vietnam.	1009–1225
China regains control of Vietnam.	1407–1427
Le Loi leads successful revolt against China, establishes the Le dynasty.	1427
Le dynasty controls Champa.	1471
Tay Son Rebellion occurs.	1788
Nguyen Long unites north and south and names it Vietnam.	1802

World History

2500 B.C.	Egyptians build the Pyramids and the Sphinx in Giza.
563 B.C.	The Buddha is born in India.
A.D. 313	The Roman emperor Constantine recognizes Christianity.
610	The Prophet Muhammad begins preaching a new religion called Islam.
1054	The Eastern (Orthodox) and Western (Roman) Churches break apart.
1066	William the Conqueror defeats the English in the Battle of Hastings.
1095	Pope Urban II proclaims the First Crusade.
1215	King John seals the Magna Carta.
1300s	The Renaissance begins in Italy.
1347	The Black Death sweeps through Europe.
1453	Ottoman Turks capture Constantinople, conquering the Byzantine Empire.
1492	Columbus arrives in North America.
1500s	The Reformation leads to the birth of Protestantism.
1776	The Declaration of Independence is signed.
1789	The French Revolution begins.

Vietnamese History

France takes control of Vietnam.	1858
France creates French Indochina.	1893
Ho Chi Minh founds Indochinese Communist Party.	1930
Japan controls Vietnam.	1940–1945
The Viet Minh nationalist organization begins fight for Vietnam's freedom.	1941
Vietnamese independence is declared.	1945
France resumes fighting for control of Vietnam.	1946
Geneva Conference divides Vietnam into North Vietnam and South Vietnam.	1954
Vietnam War begins.	1957
Ngo Dinh Diem is assassinated.	1963
United States begins bombing North Vietnam.	1964
U.S. forces begin fighting in Vietnam.	1965
Tet Offensive attacks occur on South Vietnam.	1968
United States military pulls out of Vietnam.	1973
South Vietnam surrenders to North Vietnam.	1975
The Socialist Republic of Vietnam is created.	1976
Doi moi economic reforms begin.	1986
United States ends embargo against Vietnam.	1994
Vietnam and United States establish full diplomatic relations.	1995
President Bill Clinton visits Vietnam.	2000

World History

1865	The American Civil War ends.
1914	World War I breaks out.
1917	The Bolshevik Revolution brings communism to Russia.
1929	Worldwide economic depression begins.
1939	World War II begins, following the German invasion of Poland.
1945	World War II ends.
1957	The Vietnam War starts.
1969	Humans land on the moon.
1975	The Vietnam War ends.
1979	Soviet Union invades Afghanistan.
1983	Drought and famine in Africa.
1989	The Berlin Wall is torn down, as communism crumbles in Eastern Europe.
1991	Soviet Union breaks into separate states.
1992	Bill Clinton is elected U.S. president.
2000	George W. Bush is elected U.S. president.

Fast Facts

Official name: Socialist Republic of Vietnam.
(*Cong Hoa Xa Hoi Chu Nghia Viet Nam*)

Capital: Hanoi

Official language: Vietnamese (*kinh*)

Ho Chi Minh City

Vietnam's flag

Country road

Official religion:	None
Year of founding:	1976
National anthem:	*"Tien Quan a"* (Hymn of the Marching Army)
Government:	Communist state
Chief of state:	President
Head of state:	Prime minister
Area and dimensions of country:	127,242 square miles (329,556 sq km)
Distance north to south:	1,023 miles (1,650 km)
Widest distance east to west:	372 miles (600 km)
Land and water borders:	China is to the north; Laos and Cambodia are to the west. On the east and south is the South China Sea.
Highest elevation:	Phan Si Pan, 10,312 feet (3,143 m)
Lowest elevation:	Sea level along the South China Sea coast
Highest average temperature:	85°F (29.4°C)
Lowest average temperature:	62°F (16.7°C)
Highest average annual precipitation:	78 inches (198 cm), the Mekong Delta
Lowest average annual precipitation:	66 inches (168 cm), the Red River Delta

Cave temple

Currency

National population:	76.3 million

Population of largest cities:

Ho Chi Minh City	5,200,000
Hanoi	3,300,000
Haiphong	1,500,000
Da Nang	375,000
Hue	265,000

Famous landmarks:
- ▶ ***Cu Chi Tunnels***, near Ho Chi Minh City
- ▶ ***Cao Dai Holy See***, Tay Ninh
- ▶ ***Mekong Delta***, southern Vietnam
- ▶ ***Perfume Pagoda***, southwest of Hanoi
- ▶ ***Museum of War Remnants***, Ho Chi Minh City
- ▶ ***The Marble Mountains***, south of Da Nang

Industry: Most factories produce local consumer goods. But more products are being made for export, especially textiles and processed foods such as seafood, coffee, tea, soft drinks, and condiments. Other goods that are manufactured in Vietnam include paper goods, cement, chemical fertilizers, and footwear.

Currency: The dong. 100, 200, 500, 1,000, 2,000, 5,000, 10,000, 20,000, and 50,000 notes. U.S.$1 = 14,984 dong.

Local terms:

chao	hello and goodbye
Ong/ba co khoe khong?	How are you?
Ong/ba ten gi?	What's your name?
Ten toi la…	My name is…
lam on	please
Cam on nhieu.	Thank you very much.

Schoolchildren

con gai	girl
con trai	boy
hom nay	today
mai	tomorrow
hom qua	yesterday
lue	rice
truong	school

Famous people: Ho Chi Minh (1890–1969)
Military leader and president of North Vietnam

Huynh Phu So (?–1947)
Religious leader

Nguyen Du (1765–1820)
Poet

Pham Van Dong (1906–2000)
Former prime minister, who led Vietnam's delegation to the Geneva Peace Talks in 1954

Trinh Cong Son (1939–2001)
Folk musician

Trung sisters, Trung Trac (?–A.D. 43)
and Trung Nhi
Political leaders

Tran Hieu Ngan

To Find Out More

Nonfiction

▶ Cole, Wendy M. *Vietnam*. Broomall, PA: Chelsea House, 1997.

▶ Dodd, Jan, and Mark Lewis. *Vietnam: The Rough Guide*. London: Rough Guides, 1998.

▶ Ellis, Claire. *Culture Shock! Vietnam*. Singapore: Times Books International, 1995.

▶ Hansen, Ole S. *Vietnam*. Austin, TX: Raintree/Steck Vaughn, 1997.

▶ Kalman, Bobbie. *Vietnam: The Culture*. New York: Crabtree Publishing, 1996.

▶ Parker, Lewis K. *Vietnam*. Vero Beach, FL: Rourke, 1994.

Web Sites

▶ **Vietnam's U.S. Embassy**
www.vietnamembassy-usa.org

▶ **General Vietnam information**
www.countryreports.org//content/vietnam.htm

▶ **The World Conservation Monitoring Centre, with environmental news**
www.wcmc.org.uk/infoserv/countryp/vietnam/

Embassies

▶ **Vietnamese Embassy in the United States**
1233 20th St., N.W.
Washington, DC 20036

▶ **Vietnamese Embassy in Canada**
226 Maclaren St.
Ottawa, Ontario, Canada K2P 0L9

Index

Page numbers in *italics* indicate illustrations.

Meet the Author

T ERRI WILLIS learned to love books when she was read to every day by her mother while growing up in Minnesota. "I've always loved to escape into books," she said. "Sometimes, when I was a kid, I'd be reading three or four of them at a time, and I always brought books and a flashlight under the covers with me at night."

Now, it's a thrill for her to be able to write books for a new generation of readers.

She begins researching her topic in her local library, checking out the information available there. Usually there's a lot in the reference collections and on the stacks. Encyclopedias are good starting points, too, she said, giving her a brief understanding of the topic.

From there, it becomes a matter of filling in the blanks— adding the detail that can make a book exciting and loaded with neat information. She hunts down materials from government agencies and other organizations, hits the Internet for up-to-minute facts, and sorts through the collections of

major libraries on university campuses and in large cities. "I love searching out the details," Terri said. "I especially like hanging out in big libraries. To me, it's like panning for gold. There's usually a lot to sift through, but occasionally you find that great nugget of a fact that really adds to the book."

Terri got her degree in journalism at the University of Wisconsin–Madison. She is the author of nine books for children and young adults, mostly on geography and the environment, including Enchantment of the World, *Libya* and *Romania*, and two for Children's Press Saving Planet Earth series. She's also written for a geography newsletter and several newspapers and magazines. She lives in Cedarburg, Wisconsin, with her husband, Harry, and their two young daughters, Andrea and Elizabeth, who are read to every day!

Photo Credits